SALOME'S EMBRACE

C. G. Jung, a man who accomplished a revolution in analytical psychology and made an impact both directly and indirectly on a great number of people, also took women seriously. The release of *The Red Book* has greatly added to our knowledge of Jung's relationship with the feminine: from his mother, his wife and his extramarital affairs to the effect these had on the formulation of his psychology and on the women who had the courage to explore the need for a spiritual link to Jung and who became known as the Valkyries.

In this revised and expanded study of the many women in Jung's close circle, Anthony explores the women who followed Jung during his lifetime, his need for their company, and their contributions to his work. The book includes studies of Emma Jung, Sabina Spielrein, and Toni Wolff, as well as Jung's mother Emilie, and many other collaborators and followers. It also includes chapters on *The Red Book*, the Zurich Psychological Club, and Dadaism. Including never-before published primary material, such as interviews with the women themselves, *Salome's Embrace* assesses their work and its value for the generations of Jungian analysts that have followed, including women who practice depth psychology today.

The book will be of great interest to analytical psychologists and Jungian psychotherapists in practice and in training, and to academics and students of Jungian and post-Jungian studies, gender and women's history.

Maggy Anthony studied at the C. G. Jung Institute in Zurich, Switzerland and the Zurich Clinic and Research Center for Jungian Psychology, and is a former family therapist at St. Mary's Medical Center/Maclean Center for Addictions and Behavioral Health in Nevada, USA. She is the author of several books and currently resides in Nevada.

This book arose out of Maggy Anthony's asking "what it was that kept those [Jungian] women so vital, so involved in life" well into old age. The question prompted her return to Zurich, where she had years earlier been a student at the C. G. Jung Institute. She hoped, through interviews, "to find the secrets of their older age." What she discovered resulted in this work.

In many instances women played important and dynamic roles in the furtherance of Jung's public and professional stature. Some would in time gain prominence as therapists, others as founders of psychological clubs, foundations, and institutions dedicated to the promulgation of his ideas. The maintenance and inner workings of many of these organizations was and is performed by women as well, often off-stage. Maggy Anthony's work presents the lives of some of those women, many prime movers of the Jungian community past and present, highlighting the importance of their roles and the impetus behind their dedication. She writes, "Jung, from the beginning, took women seriously, mainly perhaps because of his own psychological makeup.... He was also a very dynamic and physically attractive man ... bursting with physical and mental vitality, which made him appear a natural healer of souls."

This work covers a considerable amount of ground – from Jung's early involvement with psychology, his exchanges, and feuds with Freud, profiles of his mother, wife, and his *soror mystica* or "mystical sister," Toni Wolff. Most important are the materials gathered from Maggy Anthony's interviews and biographical sketches of the women who played (and in several instances still play) major roles in the continuance and dispersal of Jung's ideas. We learn of Jung's connection with the archetype of the Great Mother through the influence of his mother; that she too had what Jung referred to as his number one and number two personalities, an experience reaching back to his grandmother's Good Monk and Bad Monk personalities. Truly, Jung was impacted by and familiar with the feminine at a number of levels, which could easily explain why so many women flocked to work with him in one capacity or another.

The most poignant section of the work is Ms. Anthony's account of a dream she had of Jung shortly after her difficult major surgery. He said, as they stood side by side, "You must come to Switzerland; we have ancestors in common here." She would much later discover that they did share common ancestors. With two young children in tow and with little money, in the midst of a marital separation, she set sail for Switzerland. Upon arriving in Zurich, she "felt an enormous sense of homecoming, despite never having been there before." It would be the beginning of a deep journey, in which she not only resolved her post-surgery depression, but learned about the myth that had propelled her life since childhood.

Jung promoted the importance of myth for modern life. By doing so he opened an undiscovered avenue for the therapeutic process, enriching the modern individual's sense of self by connecting their psyches with the transpersonal dimension of the archetypes and the collective unconscious.

This work makes mention of many of Jung's theories, including his investigation of the esoteric topics of the *I Ching*, alchemy, and astrology, to mention a few.

A surprising and welcome part of this work is an astrological analysis of Jung's birth chart by Philip Culjak.

Any study concerned with the history of Jung's ideas and their establishment in modern thought will profit from Ms. Anthony's careful and enlightening survey of the early years of the Jungian community, and especially the support of Jungian women.

Charles Poncé, Ph.D.,
Rosebridge Graduate School, Pacifica Graduate Institute at
Santa Barbara, and the San Francisco Art Institute, USA

SALOME'S EMBRACE

The Jungian Women

Maggy Anthony

Routledge
Taylor & Francis Group
LONDON AND NEW YORK

First published 2018
by Routledge
2 Park Square, Milton Park, Abingdon, Oxon OX14 4RN

and by Routledge
711 Third Avenue, New York, NY 10017

Routledge is an imprint of the Taylor & Francis Group, an informa business

© 2018 Maggy Anthony

The right of Maggy Anthony to be identified as author of this work has been asserted by her in accordance with sections 77 and 78 of the Copyright, Designs and Patents Act 1988.

All rights reserved. No part of this book may be reprinted or reproduced or utilised in any form or by any electronic, mechanical, or other means, now known or hereafter invented, including photocopying and recording, or in any information storage or retrieval system, without permission in writing from the publishers.

Trademark notice: Product or corporate names may be trademarks or registered trademarks, and are used only for identification and explanation without intent to infringe.

British Library Cataloguing in Publication Data
A catalogue record for this book is available from the British Library

Library of Congress Cataloguing in Publication Data
Names: Anthony, Maggy, author.
Title: Salome's embrace : the Jungian women / Maggy Anthony.
Description: Abingdon, Oxon ; New York, NY : Routledge, 2018. | Includes bibliographical references.
Identifiers: LCCN 2017026345 (print) | LCCN 2017039026 (ebook) | ISBN 9781315226316 (Master e-Book) | ISBN 9780415787208 (hardback) | ISBN 9780415787215 (pbk.)
Subjects: LCSH: Jung, C. G. (Carl Gustav), 1875–1961–Friends and associates. | Psychoanalysts–Austria–Biography. | Psychoanalysis–History. | Jungian psychology–History.
Classification: LCC BF109.J8 (ebook) | LCC BF109.J8 A683 2018 (print) | DDC 150.1954092–dc23
LC record available at https://lccn.loc.gov/2017026345

ISBN: 978-0-415-78720-8 (hbk)
ISBN: 978-0-415-78721-5 (pbk)
ISBN: 978-1-315-22631-6 (ebk)

Typeset in Bembo
by Out of House Publishing
Printed and bound by CPI Group (UK) Ltd, Croydon, CR0 4YY

This book is dedicated to
Andrea Thorsen Turman
Friend Mentor Ally
And to the memory of
Bettilou C. O'Leary
1929–1972
Sarava Iemanja!

CONTENTS

Preface		*xi*
Acknowledgements		*xiv*

	Introduction	1
1	The beginning: opening to the world	5
2	Mother: Emilie Preiswerk Jung	11
3	The beginnings of the entourage: Emma Jung	14
4	Siegfried's mate: Sabina Spielrein	21
5	The fragrance: Toni Wolff	29
6	Zurich Psychological Club: Edith Rockefeller McCormick	37
7	Art attack: dancing with the Dadaists	40
8	Sieglinde: Linda Fierz-David	46
9	The mysteries of woman: M. Esther Harding	51
10	The Americans: Eleanor Bertine and Kristine Mann	56

11 Eranos: Olga Fröbe-Kapteyn   59

12 The alchemist's daughter: Marie-Louise von Franz   63

13 Impresaria: Jolande Jacobi   68

14 Priestess: Dion Fortune   73

15 The veiled lady of visions: Christiana Morgan   77

16 The rest of the entourage   80
    Barbara Hannah: daughter of the cathedral close 80
    Dr. Elizabeth Osterman: transformation 81
    Dora Kalff: sand dreams 83
    Mary Foote's notes 84
    Mary Bancroft: the spy who loved him 86
    Hilde Kirsch: the exile 87
    Lucile Elliott: the dreamer 88

17 Jung: the *animus mundi*   91

18 The Jungian women: an assessment   98

19 She Who Remembers   101

20 Into the future   113
    The battle of the animus 113
    Jungian women of the twenty-first century 114
    Jungian women in the first half of life 118

21 The *hieros gamos*   120

Appendix 1: Jung's birth chart by Philip Culjak   *123*
Appendix 2: Timeline: C. G. Jung and the Jungian women   *131*
Author biography   *133*
Index   *134*

PREFACE

In this year of 2017, I find myself once more looking back to my year of studies at the C. G. Jung Institute in Zurich – forty years ago – and to the beginnings of this book, which, very properly, began with my meeting those Jungian women, known mostly affectionately as the Valkyries. It was only five years after my studies in Zurich that, faced with my mother dying, I began to wonder what it was that kept those women so vital, so involved in life at the same age as my mother, who had become bitter and angry in her last years. And in that wondering came the idea for me to return to Zurich, to talk to them and to find the secrets of their older age.

The year was 1977 and there was in America, following the cultural explosions of the late 1960s, a renewed interest in Carl Jung and all things Jungian. Upon my mother's death that year, I took my two children, Anna and Joshua, and myself off to one of America's sacred places, Mount Shasta, to live for the summer. Once there, I began to meditate on just what I wanted to know from the Jungian women. I realized the "secret" I wanted to uncover was the source of their continued engagement with life into their eighties and nineties. I realized that I wanted to know this not only to understand my mother's anger and bitterness in old age, but as guidance for my own aging as I turned forty that year.

So, in the shadow of that mountain – so revered through the ages by the Native Americans who lived nearby, and also in modern times by spiritual seekers from as far away as Mongolia – I made a pilgrimage to it.

The idea for a book began to take shape and I finally sent a proposal to a literary agent in New York. At the time, I had few financial resources to even consider a trip back to Zurich, let alone for staying to interview and to research the early days of Jung and the women who gathered around him to be healed and had stayed on to heal others. These women had come from all over the world, beginning at the time of the First World War, from America, from Germany, from England, from Palestine. Once there, the charisma of Jung and his thought, which took the feminine seriously for the first time, induced them to want to share it with others through analysis and through their writing. Later on, they shared it through teaching at the Institute created in his name.

To my surprise, an American publisher accepted the proposal for my book almost immediately, and I was pushed to make preparations for a trip back to Zurich to speak with the women firsthand.

My first impulse was to contact Dr. James Yandell, who had been my analyst for several years and had been a mentor too, encouraging my dreams and interests. He had several suggestions for interviewing the Jungians in California, both men and women, who he felt were essential to my research, in preparation for the Zurich crowd. It took me the rest of that year to do those interviews in the San Francisco Bay Area and Los Angeles. The interviews were conducted mainly in the company of my long-time friend, Stephen Kathriner, an art educator who had the experience of a Jungian analysis and who agreed to assist with setting up my recording device and to be an introverted presence to my extraverted intuitive one. I was very grateful for his presence, as I was nervous to approach such illustrious names in the field of Jungian psychology: Dr. Joseph Henderson, Dr. Joseph Wheelwright and his wife, Jane Wheelwright, among others. The interviews went smoothly, with many anecdotes of firsthand experiences of the Valkyries being shared by all. Once the California interviews were completed in the spring of 1978, I made preparations for my children and me to once more travel to Zurich.

First though, I felt it only proper to share the interview outlines I had written with a few of the people whom I had interviewed. I was very surprised, to say the least, when one of those interviewees, a woman, became very upset, claiming she didn't realize I was going to use what she and her husband had said in their interviews. This, after having helped me find an outlet to plug in my recorder and set it up so the microphone was in front of them. She was furious I was writing anything at all concerning Jung; after all, who was I to presume to do so? Then in a *coup de grâce*, she vowed to contact the women she knew in Zurich to warn them of my arrival, which she did, making a person-to-person interview with them difficult, and in some cases impossible. At this point I was once again glad for the presence of my friend Stephen at those first interviews to reassure me I had not somehow incurred the wrath of this person due to some clumsiness of questioning or arrogance on my part. I was truly baffled about why she would lash out so vehemently.

As it was, once in Zurich, I began my interviews with those women who were willing to participate, with questions regarding Jung and his psychology: the reasons he and it had attracted the women in the first place; whether this depth psychology had anything to do with their longevity and vitality; and what myths had made their presence felt in the analytical relationship with him.

I had not anticipated their almost universal introversion. In Jungian terms, most of the women, with the exception of Jolande Jacobi, who sadly had died before I arrived back, were deeply introverted. Many of the most generalized questions were regarded as invasions of privacy. The most often used phrase was "I will talk to you about Jung, but I will not discuss anything personal." And of course, the communication received by some from the Jungian woman in California didn't help.

Of course, material from and about the women themselves was to be augmented, researched, and rooted out from various writings in Jungian journals, obituaries, and memoirs from a variety of sources. Because of a lack of publicly available published material on some at the time, Aniela Jaffé, Liliane Frey-Rohn, and others were regretfully left out. Less reticent to speak were many of the Jungian men, who noted, sometimes humorously, sometimes with resentment, the interplay between Jung and the women. Also at that time, 1978, Jung's family determined that personal information about their father and grandfather should not become public.

My original book, *The Valkyries: The Women around Jung*, was eventually published in 1990; a revised edition, *Jung's Circle of Women: The Valkyries*, was released in 1999. This current book, *Salome's Embrace: The Jungian Women*, is a vastly expanded edition, generously enriched by the availability of new research and subsequent publications, including, of course, the release of Jung's *The Red Book* and other personal material, thanks in large measure to the willingness and generosity of Jung's family to further share with the world.

So much of this book, of course, also comes from anecdotal material told in a friendly atmosphere during those early interviews, from the psychology of Jung himself, and from reading between the lines of written accounts of certain festivities and meetings. And as time has gone on and the major players of the early days are now all deceased, more information about these incredible Jungian women is becoming available in books and articles. And now, I find myself of an age the Valkyries were themselves when I interviewed them so many years ago, and this has brought, I hope and believe, more understanding on my part.

It is largely because of my own admiration for the bulk of Jung's psychology, and my identification with so much of what he found through his own journey, that I "dared" to write this book at all, and now have enlarged and brought more thought to this current incarnation of it, especially in the advent of the publishing of *The Red Book*.

And now – forty-five years after the first dream I had of Jung, which urged me to study at the Zurich Institute – may I dare to hope that Jung himself might be interested, since he came into my dreams three more times during the writing of this book, and in the last dream was waiting impatiently at a blackboard for me to give birth so he could mark it down on a chart on which he had sketched five stars, the final one of which was not yet colored in …

ACKNOWLEDGEMENTS

I wish to thank my dear brother, Lou O'Leary, for sending me *Memories, Dreams, Reflections* while I was living in Rio de Janeiro, thus changing the course of my life, and following that up with the *Collected Works* of C. G. Jung and, most recently, *The Red Book*. His and my sister-in-law Judith Graves O'Leary's support has been steady and caring.

And my now adult children, Joshua Anthony and Anna Krave, for traveling while very young to foreign lands and living there with me uncomplainingly (most of the time). They were my biggest support system and have remained so throughout the writing of this book.

To my very good friend, Andrea Thorsen Turman, whose assistance during the year of writing this book has been invaluable. I don't know that I would have attempted it without her, and our conversations have certainly enriched this book.

To Professor Paul Bishop, William Jacks Chair in Modern Languages, University of Glasgow, Scotland, for his encouragement and referral to Routledge as a possible publisher for this new edition of my work on the Jungian women, *Salome's Embrace*.

Continuing gratitude to my old friend, Stephen Kathriner, who in our weekly telephone talks and frequent visits offered a good ear for what I had to say, and made many good suggestions, and the loan of some useful books.

To Dr. Oliver Ocskay, for being there when I had questions to ask about Jungian matters, and for being a good friend.

To Dr. Peter Kingsley, for his deep and erudite scholarship and impeccable writing – he is an inspiration.

To my niece, Dr. Renee O'Leary, for obtaining through her research several key documents for me.

To my good friend, John Roth, for alerting me to several Jungian women he heard lecture at Pacifica Graduate Institute in Santa Barbara, sending me links to contact them.

Also to my three Jungian analysts, Dr. John N. K. Langton, Dr.med. Heinrich Fierz, and Dr. James Yandell, none of whom ever spoke the word "animus" and all of whom encouraged me in following my dreams and pursuits. This has been true too of my analyst, Dr. Charles Poncé, who got me writing again, and of Dr. Julius Rogina, who kept me steady and on course these past couple of years.

Finally, to those wonderful Jungian women, whose example in living and working gave me a blueprint for living and for my own older age, which has served me well. I give thanks for their lives, which have had an impact on so many others as well.

INTRODUCTION

Anyone attempting to write about the renowned Swiss psychiatrist and psychoanalyst Carl Gustav Jung and his relationship to the women whom he counseled and with whom he worked and engaged on so many levels, if writing before the publication of Jung's *The Red Book* in 2009, will have had a sad lack of critical information essential to that subject. At least that has been my belief and experience.

Jung himself felt that the reading of *The Red Book* was critical to the understanding of the development of his theory of what has come to be called analytical psychology. It is my contention that the reading of it is an important key to the understanding of Jung himself, particularly regarding his relationship to the feminine and his concept of the anima. And a key to the impact of his psychology and himself on the women known variously as the Valkyries, the Jungfrauen, and other semi-serious titles.

I have written elsewhere (Anthony 1999) that the fact of being born a Swiss man in 1875 came with its own assumptions and attitudes regarding women. This was a time when women were largely categorized as household angels, temptresses, or occasionally as muses in more elevated and artistic circles. In any case, they were not to be taken too seriously. In Jung's writings and interviews regarding women, most of the prejudices of the age show through, even as late as 1955, when he said in an interview, "A man's foremost interest should be his work. But a woman – man is her work and her business" (McGuire and Hull 1987, p. 244).

In his actual therapeutic and personal contact with the women, this was not always the case. Of the women in this book I was privileged to interview many years ago, almost all of them spoke of feeling "freed" by their analysis and association with him. Several spoke of being taken seriously for the first time. I began to wonder how much of this was due to their sensing unconscious aspects of Jung, despite his insistence on being neither artist nor mystic. Both of these are questionable assertions, particularly in light of the publication of *The Red Book*. He seemed very fearful of not being taken seriously within the sciences.

> The publication of the *Red Book* prompts one to ask how the image of the Jung that arises from the illuminated pages may be reconciled with the image of a Jung who held that "psychology constituted the fundamental scientific discipline, upon which other disciplines should henceforth be based."
>
> (Bishop 2013, p. 15, citing Shamdasani 2003)

The very artistry and image making that went into the construction of *The Red Book* seem contradictory to a "fundamental scientific discipline."

In my reading of *The Red Book* and particularly of the vision Jung had with Elijah and Salome, I was struck by his later commentaries on it in which he seemed to fall short in his interpretation, to me, especially of the figure of Salome. He seemed to brush aside Elijah's comment that "My wisdom and my daughter are one" and to regard her as some evil temptress, despite that comment. "Salome denotes bad qualities. She brings to mind … the murder of the holy one" (Jung 2009, p. 566). He was looking at her in her specific existence in the Bible, and not as a being whose symbolic role was perhaps not that cut and dried. And of course, the *fin-de-siècle* obsession with the figure of Salome herself, which was demonstrated abundantly in many paintings of the period by major artists, had its own influence. The impact of Oscar Wilde's play *Salome* in 1894 was enormous, as was that of the opera based on his play written by Richard Strauss, which was performed in Zurich in 1907.[1] Whether Jung saw it or not, the publicity surrounding such a "scandalous" play would have filled the newspapers. "As the nineteenth century gave way to the twentieth, a short-lived but extraordinary phenomenon spread throughout Europe and the United States – 'Salomania.' The term was coined when biblical bad girl Salome was resurrected from the Old Testament and reborn" (Bentley 2002, dust jacket). The play and the opera wreak havoc with the original story, leaving out some key elements and making Salome pure evil temptress. In the Bible it is clear that it is Salome's mother who instructs her to ask her stepfather for the head of John the Baptist.

Actually it was in the New Testament, and in it (Mark 15:40) Salome is present with the Virgin Mary and two other Marys at the death of Jesus on the Cross, though it is not clear if this was *the* Salome. In addition, modern feminist writers, writing of Goddess spirituality, insist the infamous Dance of the Seven Veils was actually an acting out of the death of the sacred king and his descent into the Underworld, with the Goddess, to eventual rebirth (Walker 1983).

However, it was the Salome of the imagination of the *fin-de-siècle* artists and writers who was coming into play when Jung was a young man in his twenties. As a historian of the period has written, "In the turn of the century imagination, the figure of Salome epitomized the inherent perversity of women: their eternal circularity and their ability to destroy the male's soul even while they remained nominally chaste in body" (Spano 2013). This might provide an answer to the question Claire

Douglas asks in her splendid book on women and analytical psychology, "Why was Jung suspicious of Salome, his own inner feminine and how did that distrust come about?" (Douglas 2000, p. 24).

In his *Memories, Dreams, Reflections*, Jung himself admits to an early distrust of women, pointing to his mother's absence, felt as a desertion, during a prolonged hospitalization when he was quite young. However, it was the figure of a young housekeeper who filled in the role partially, and by his own admission, provided his earliest anima image (Hillman 1985/2007, p. 27). Interestingly, her physical description mirrors that of the women of his earliest extramarital affairs, Sabina Spielrein and Toni Wolff.

> She had black hair and an olive complexion, and was quite different from my mother. I can see, even now, her hairline, her throat, with its darkly pigmented skin, and her ear. All this seemed to me very strange and yet strangely familiar ... it was as though she belonged ... only to me, as though she were connected in some way with other mysterious things I could not understand. This type of girl later became a component of my anima.
>
> *(Jung 1989, p. 8)*

In commenting on the Elijah/Salome vision in *The Red Book*, Matthew Spano states, "the *Red Book* has an element of incompletion, even tragedy of Jung's inability to completely love and trust his soul and thereby develop fully this immature part of his personality" (Spano 2013).

As the writing and visions go on, I was also struck by Elijah more or less becoming Philemon, unaccompanied by his partner Baucis, but later paired with Salome. As more commentaries by other Jungians came out after its publication I could see I was not alone in this observation. "Curiously ... Jung completely omits Baucis and opts not to draw upon the defining characteristics of their story – i.e. their marital intimacy, fidelity, and love" (Spano 2013). Might this indicate that the seductive Salome is the anima figure, much distrusted, but much desired, while the wifely Baucis is left out and unexamined?

Later, in the drafts of the *Liber Novus*, some of which were written in the 1920s, there is a strong indication that Jung finally was coming, or had come, to terms with the figure of Salome. In note 197 in the Reader's Edition of *The Red Book*, Jung wrote: "As a thinker, I had rejected my feeling but I had rejected part of life ... it then became apparent that Salome, i.e. my pleasure, was my soul" (Jung 2009, p. 190).

All this led me to re-examine how this might have shaped the lives and work of the women who were close to Jung, wrote their own books, and lectured on Jungian psychology, but most of whom did not seem to take further his ideas from their own experiences as women. The few who did will be noted.

Note

1 Information on the performance of the opera *Salome* by Richard Strauss in Zurich was provided by John Roth and www.opernhaus.ch/en/our-history. Many thanks.

References

Anthony, Maggy (1999) *Jung's Circle of Women: The Valkyries*. York Beach, Maine: Nicholas-Hays.
Bentley, Toni (2002) *Sisters of Salome*. New Haven and London: Yale University Press.
Bishop, Paul (2013) "Jung and the Quest for Beauty: The *Red Book* in Relation to German Classicism." In *The Red Book: Reflections on C. G. Jung's Liber Novus*, Thomas Kirsch and George Hogenson, eds. Abingdon: Routledge, pp. 11–35.
Douglas, Claire (2000) *The Woman in the Mirror: Analytical Psychology and the Feminine*. Lincoln, Nebraska: iUniverse. First published Boston: Sigo Press, 1990.
Hillman, James (1985/2007) *Anima: An Anatomy of a Purified Notion*. Dallas, Texas: Spring Books.
Jung, C. G. (1989) *Memories, Dreams, Reflections*. New York: Vintage Books.
Jung, C. G. (2009) *The Red Book: The Reader's Edition*, ed. Sonu Shamdasani. New York: W. W. Norton.
McGuire, William and Hull, R. F. C., eds. (1987) *C. G. Jung Speaking: Interviews and Encounters*. Princeton, New Jersey: Princeton University Press.
Shamdasani, Sonu (2003) *Jung and the Making of a Modern Psychology*. New York: Cambridge University Press.
Spano, Matthew V. (2013) "*The Red Book*: Some Notes for the Beginner." *The Jung Page: Reflections on Psychology, Culture and Life*, October 27, www.cgjungpage.org/learn/articles/analytical-psychology/928-the-red-book-some-notes-for-the-beginner.
Walker, Barbara G. (1983) *The Woman's Encyclopedia of Myths and Secrets*. New York: Harper & Row.

1
THE BEGINNING
Opening to the world

In the fall of 1948 in Zurich, after more than thirty years of working in the protected atmosphere of the Psychological Club as a small, closely knit, if sometimes contentious group, shielded from an often confused and hostile public, Jung and his circle opened the doors to the world. It was an exciting day, but the excitement was expressed in that repressed way which is very Swiss. The old building on the Gemeindestrasse with the staid Victorian exterior seemed to belie the momentousness of the occasion. Symbolically, the doors opened, not onto the street, but into a small, sheltered courtyard that had to be entered from the sidewalk. It was located in the realm of the gods,

> where it runs past Minervastrasse (the street of the Goddess of Wisdom) and the Neptunestrasse (the street of the God of the Sea – in Jung's psychology, often a symbol of the unconscious) and not far away are Mercurstrasse (the street of Mercury, deity much discussed by Jung), and the Heliostrasse, and the Lunastrasse (the streets of the Sun and the Moon which, Zurich geography imitating alchemical tradition, merge), and Wotanstrasse (the street … related to … Dionysus).
>
> *(Bishop 1994, p. 95)*

As each student pressed the outside bell, Fraulein Amman would come to the massive wooden door, open it cautiously and enquire as to who was there, and what was the nature of their business. It must have seemed rather more like requesting an audience with the Pope than attending a place of higher education. The confused accents of the young American students, the Schweitzer-Deutsch of the Zurich students, and the more formal High German of the doctors and professors swept over the impassive countenance of this human watchdog as she conducted them into a small classroom inside. Fraulein Amman would then retire to the tiny kitchen and begin preparations for the coffee to be served midway through the class.

Every once in a while, the secretary, Fraulein Aniela Jaffé, would peek nervously into the subdued classroom to see if all were gathered yet.

At last the door opened and Frau Jolande Jacobi, a petite, well-dressed woman of middle age, walked in and went to the podium. She glanced nervously at the twelve students who had gathered and seated themselves, somewhat defensively, at the back of the classroom. She smiled a bit tremulously at them and said, "Please. Come to the front of the room. I'm an extravert and I like to have people around me." In spite of the obvious strength that emanated from her, it was apparent she needed the support of the students. Reluctantly they gathered their books and papers, slowly making their ways to the front of the classroom. The first day of the C. G. Jung Institute for Analytical Psychology had begun.

In the weeks that followed, nervousness was the dominant feature of the teaching staff, which was made up of those women who were part of the inner circle around Jung, most from the earliest days of his career. The nervousness was due to the fact that for the first time they were presenting material to people outside their charmed circle. The composition of the teaching staff changed over the years as new teachers came in and others returned to their home countries to spread the Jungian word. But in general, they were known to the students by several irreverent nicknames: the Vestal Virgins, the Maenads, the Jungfrauen, and the Valkyries.

According to one of the many American students of the early days of the Institute, nervousness seemed out of character in these otherwise intellectually formidable women. However, in retrospect, it can be appreciated that the business of becoming public, after Jung and his thought had been almost a family affair for decades previously, would almost certainly make for tension. The fact there had been so much in-fighting and hurt feelings as the Institute was being formed certainly didn't help. Toni Wolff was left out, as was Linda Fierz-David, and Dr. Jacobi, who was not much liked by the others, ultimately got her way in so much of the planning. Not to mention she was given a place on the Curatorium despite the protests of many of the others.

Jung had the last word in many matters concerning the framework. "When the Institute was founded in 1948, [Jung] said the institute was a research center with teaching of certain basic things such as anthropology and folklore. It was not a training institute" (Hillman and Shamdasani 2013, p. 144). Over the years that followed, much of that changed. However, shortly after Jung's seventieth birthday on July 26, 1945, he had told Jacobi to go to Geneva to prepare a study on how best to found an institute in Zurich. He apparently said to her, "We have all these old ladies here, all sick people … only cured or half-cured patients but no scientists" (Bair 2003, pp. 506–507). He was obviously anxious that the institute would be intellectually sound. And that was perhaps why he insisted on her having a role in it. Also, he felt that as an extravert, she would have greater means of communicating with the outside world.

Jung himself chose the first Curatorium, or Board of Directors. On it he put two men, C. A. Meier and Ludwig Binswanger, both distinguished analysts. He chose two of the more outgoing women as the other members: Dr. Jacobi and Liliane Frey-Rohn. There was a great deal of controversy over his choice of Dr. Jacobi. As we shall later see, she was not popular among the members of the Zurich Psychological Club. After much challenging, Jung had his way, naturally, claiming she was the most adept of them all in dealing with the public. Dr. Joseph Henderson referred to her as the Sol Hurok of Jungian affairs, and maintained she was the most exasperating woman, who grated on the nerves of the more introverted Jungians (Henderson 1977). Perhaps there was a small amount of jealousy over her natural ability to charm people. Difficult or not, much of the Institute was created from her prodigious energies.

It soon became evident that the Institute was a showcase for the variety of talents and personalities of the women around Jung. And, more than any of his male contemporaries, it was women who were particularly drawn to his work and personality. Some reasons for this were more apparent than others. One major reason was that in the early twentieth century, women were still very much second-class citizens. As Dr. Liliane Frey-Rohn put it, "Women were still thought to be without souls" (Frey-Rohn 1978). Few creative men, during the first half of that century, took women seriously at all, still less would men willingly take them on as collaborators or assistants as Jung did, though they might just find them useful as muses.

Jung, from the beginning, took women seriously, mainly perhaps because of his own psychological makeup, as we shall see. He wrote an article in 1927 titled "Woman in Europe," which was to attract many of his female followers in spite of such now-obviously sexist remarks as, "But no one can get around the fact that by taking up a masculine profession, studying and working like a man, woman is doing something not wholly in accord with, if not directly injurious, to her feminine nature." And, "It is a woman's outstanding characteristic that she can do anything for the love of a man. But those women who achieve something important for the love of a THING are most exceptional, because this does not agree with their nature. Love for a thing is a man's prerogative" (Jung 1970, pp. 117 and 118). These remarks must be taken in the context of the time and of the very traditional Swiss culture from which he came.

He was also a very dynamic and physically attractive man, and this cannot be underestimated as part of his power. He was bursting with physical and mental vitality, which made him appear a natural healer of souls. "Von Franz was overwhelmed by the towering Jung, many years later she recalled how she fell for him in a terrific transference and a big schoolgirl crush" (Bair 2003, p. 369). And, "Although Jung was twenty-eight years older than I was, I found him an extremely attractive man. Tall, with a large, healthy frame and a handsome rather leonine head, Jung exuded health and vigor" (Bancroft 1983, p. 92).

These, and many other impressions of Jung from women encountering him for the first time, seem reminiscent of Walter Otto's description of Dionysus as an "indestructible" life force. Also Jung's personal psychology must be taken into consideration, which made him particularly vulnerable and open to the feminine, though wary.

From the beginnings of his private practice, Jung had a disproportionately large number of women patients. Although the aforementioned attractiveness played its part, another reason may have been his difficulties in relating to men. He admits this in a letter to Freud (McGuire 1974). Many of the Jungian men I interviewed felt he was an overwhelming figure, whose sheer force of personality and stature made them feel unimportant. Most of the men got away as soon as possible so their own lights could shine.

The women came as patients and many remained as analysts, colleagues, or helpers of one sort or another, particularly the unmarried ones. Jung's vitality, good looks, and impression of being larger than life did not threaten them, and merely added to their attachment to him. He was also very much in touch, through his important, if difficult relationship to his mother, with what is described in Jungian thought as the feminine side of his nature, or anima, which had its shadowy and negative side too. Observers have said he was very aware of his effect upon women and felt it entailed a responsibility from which he never tried to escape. It might also be said he never did anything to discourage it. "He never let you down" (Wheelwright, Jane 1977). He did hold to the view prevalent at that time that women related to life solely through men. However, he did feel it was important for women to have their own work, though one has the impression that often this was to prevent the full force of the mother's and wife's energies focusing on the husband and children to their detriment. The fear of women was in Jung too.

As a young American man, Joe Wheelwright, coming to Jung shortly before the Second World War, was indignant about the women who seemed to form a human cordon around Jung. Wheelwright said something to Jung to the effect that he didn't see how Jung could stand "those old girls" fluttering around him. Jung became very angry and told him that every one of the women was doing important and creative work and that not only were they a help to him, but they were furthering the knowledge and understanding of psychology. His psychology. He went on to say they had come to him when they had not been able to function well, but now they could. He admitted they seemed to need a lifeline to him and that as long as he saw them once every three months, six months or a year, they could function well. He added that he loved and respected these women, even though it was a burden being the spiritual father who energized them, and he kept them in equilibrium so they could keep on doing their good work. "Wait until you are my age, and if you don't have a few of these 'old girls' hanging around, I'll be surprised … and by that time you will have changed your attitude toward them" (Wheelwright, Joseph 1977).

This reveals much about Jung and his attitude to the women around him. From the journal of another man we hear that "Unkind gossip has accused these disciples and auditors of snobbery. But when someone raised the objection that a majority of his disciples were women, Jung is said to have replied, 'What's to be done? Psychology after all is the science of the soul, and it is not my fault that the soul is a woman.'" A jest; but for anyone who has followed his teachings, a jest which is itself charged with experience.

All this suggests that Jung knew the women needed his presence, even if only in the form of an occasional visit, for their continued well-being. This is a very shamanistic view in its acceptance that the very physical presence of the healer is capable of healing. It suggests, too, that the transference (whereby the analysand works out unresolved conflicts on the analyst) was never completely abandoned nor did Jung expect it to be. One begins to wonder to what degree it was mutual; did Jung need these women's support as much as they needed his? What of his counter-transference?

Jung, following in the classic humanist tradition, needed his *femme inspiratrice*, or creative muse. He lived in the same cultural tradition as did his "ancestor" Goethe, and still called upon women as sources of inspiration and called upon them from his early days at the Burgholzli, especially with Sabina Spielrein.

Jung's psychology stems from an awareness of the mythic material operating in the psyche. There are strong indications that one of the myths operating in his own personality was that of Dionysus, indications of which cropped up regularly in the women's descriptions of him. Mention is made of the fact he was adept at helping women patients find themselves and their "greater personalities." When they dreamed of him as a wizard or wise old man, he would say, "Good! Excellent! Now that you have dreamed it, it shows you have the potential within yourself!" As Jane Wheelwright put it, "With Jung you didn't have to be someone famous or special or unusual. He treated you as if you *were* special" (Wheelwright, Jane 1977). At a time when ambitious women were frowned upon and not encouraged, even felt to be somewhat unnatural, Jung realized they needed intellectual outlets. This is very Dionysian, as the God would arouse women, in the ancient legends, to leave home and hearth, and come out into the world and dance.

To find the true beginnings of the circle of women, which formed around him, we must go to Jung's early days of fascination with woman and the role she played in man's psyche. Seen psychologically, this undoubtedly began with his mother, Emilie Preiswerk Jung.

References

Bair, Deirdre (2003) *Jung: A Biography*. Boston: Little, Brown.
Bancroft, Mary (1983) *Autobiography of a Spy*. New York: Wm. Morrow & Co.
Bishop, Paul (1994) "The Members of Jung's Zarathustra Seminar." *Spring: A Journal of Archetype and Culture* 56: 92–122.
Frey-Rohn, Liliane (June 1978) Author's interview.
Henderson, Joseph (November 1977) Author's interview.
Hillman, James and Shamdasani, Sonu (2013) *Lament of the Dead: Psychology after Jung's Red Book*. New York: W. W. Norton.

Jung, C. G. (1970) "Woman in Europe." In *Civilization in Transition*, trans. R. F. C. Hull. New York: Routledge, pp. 113–133.

McGuire, William, ed. (1974) *The Freud–Jung Letters*. Princeton, New Jersey: Princeton University Press.

Wheelwright, Jane (November 1977) Author's interview.

Wheelwright, Joseph (November 1977) Author's interview.

2
MOTHER
Emilie Preiswerk Jung

In our world cultures for the past 2,000 years, we have only the human mother who stands alone, seemingly taking all the blame and praise for the raising of her children. Before that, behind her was the archetypal Great Mother, who carried some of her burden.

In Jung's psychology the biological mother is important, but behind her stands the primordial Mother. Jung was particularly conscious of both figures in his personal life. His mother, Emilie Preiswerk Jung, often stood in the shadow of the archetypal Goddess in her son's eyes, which is evident in his earliest memory of her.

"One [memory] recalls a slender young woman wearing a dress made of black printed all over with green crescents, who could be happy and laughing, but was subject to fits of depression" (Brome 2001, p. 6). One is tempted to linger on that memory of the dress with its associations to lunar Goddesses around the world and even the figure of Luna in alchemy, which was Jung's major study from 1928 to the end of his life.

Jung's mother dominates his memoir, *Memories, Dreams, Reflections*. Much less is written about his father, who seems a shadowy, sad figure who brooded over his religion and was discontent. Emilie, in contrast, had two dominant personalities, referred to as such by Jung – one the pleasant, daytime mother, and the other the Night Mother who was full of stories about the psychic events in her family, and who herself seemed forbidding and mysterious, full of a dark knowledge not expressed by day. This personality spoke with the voice of a sibyl and was unexpectedly powerful, "a somber, imposing figure, possessed of an unmistakable authority and no bones about it" (Jung 1989, p. 48). This second personality seems to share the qualities of a woman of ancient times, an almost mythological being. In his writings, Jung states that encounters with the archetypes sometime take place in high-flown language and archaic speech; an appearance of the archetype of the Great Mother.

12   Mother: Emilie Preiswerk Jung

What Jung does not mention was that Emilie's own mother spoke of having two personalities within herself, the Good Monk and the Bad Monk. And her husband actually researched them and maintained they had been real persons. She also experienced a sort of waking sleep in which she prophesied. Emilie's father, Samuel Preiswerk, was hardly a typical parson. Beside an obsession with the idea of Zion, and his Hebrew studies, triggered perhaps by his idea that Hebrew was the language spoken in heaven, he regularly practiced psychism of a rather singular sort. He spoke to his first wife every week at clairvoyant sessions, while his second wife, mother of his twelve children, including Emilie, looked on. The fact that his second wife was not particularly thrilled with the idea probably created a psychic atmosphere of its own.

Later on, Emilie was required by her father to stand behind his chair while he worked, to protect him from ghosts, or demons, who might sneak up from behind. Obviously, though he trafficked with spirits, he was not altogether comfortable with them. What Emilie was to do in the event of such an attack was never made clear. Perhaps her virginity was thought to be enough to keep them from putting in an appearance. Certainly her father's expectations of such invasions would make an indelible impression on the psyche of a child, whether she "saw" anything or not. Thus in addition to her mother's second sight and seizures, it becomes understandable that Emilie developed a second personality of an uncanny nature, which certainly impressed itself on her son.

Jung wrote of knowing even when quite young, "it occurred to me that I was actually two different persons. One of them was a schoolboy and the other was important, a high authority … an old man who lived in the eighteenth century" (Jung 1989, p. 48).

Many years later, the New York analyst Erlo van Waveren said that Jung told him he believed in reincarnation. "I once spoke to Professor Jung about [reincarnation] and later his wife came up to me and said, 'Don't talk to anyone about this, the time isn't ripe for it yet'" (quoted in Cott 1987, pp. 200–204). And later, "Now that I myself am in my eighties, I can tell you that Professor Jung informed me that he had come back every hundred years since the thirteenth century" (quoted in Cott 1987, pp. 200–204). One wonders if Jung came to believe that the old eighteenth-century man was one of his previous incarnations.

One of Jung's first papers in psychology was based on yet more psychic happenings from the maternal side of his family: his observation and participation in séances with a young, mediumistic cousin. The paper was entitled "On the Psychology and Pathology of So-called Occult Phenomena." These experiments were conducted with Helene Preiswerk (his cousin on his mother's side) and attended by Jung and his mother among other family members. Though not directly named in the paper, Helene's participation leaked out and she became considered "unmarriageable" in the town where she lived and was sent to France to learn needlework. A few years later she died of tuberculosis.

How much of his mother's own psychism might have been linked to the repressions of a vital young woman with no intellectual outlets, married to a sad dreamy man who felt his best years were behind him, was never speculated on by Jung. Undoubtedly it added to his later insights in the treatment of the women who were to come to him to whom he suggested study and intellectual pursuits.

The degree of sublimation of Emilie Jung's energies is indicated in the fact that at one point she had to enter a hospital for the treatment of an unspecified illness. Hysteria was suggested later on by Sabina Spielrein. Various biographies of Jung suggest this might have been a mental breakdown. More often it is the body that breaks down in the form of a somatic complaint under the pressures and repressions of the mind, and serves up a physical illness that will take place of an actual mental breakdown. Jung was obviously marked by this absence, as he makes clear when he recollects eighty years later, "I was deeply troubled by my mother's being away. From then on I was always mistrustful when the word 'love' was spoken" (Jung 1989, p. 48) And, one wonders, "woman" as well?

Animals, trees, and running water – these images put us in the presence and domain of the Great Mother, rather than the Judeo-Christian God. And Emilie keeps this pagan quality throughout her son's autobiography. He continued to associate his mother with paganism rather than the Christian faith right up to her death in 1922, when he was forty-seven years old. On the night of her death he had a dream rooted in Teutonic mythology. He goes on to interpret this dream in accordance with what he felt to be his mother's rootedness in a tradition that predates ordinary Christian morality (Jung 1989, p. 48). Undoubtedly it was this strong relationship with his mother, and through her to the archetypal feminine, which colored all his future relationships with women and in his theories of the anima and the feminine.

References

Brome, Vincent (2001) *Jung: Man and Myth*. Looe, UK: House of Stratus.
Cott, Jonathan (1987) *The Search for Omm Sety*. New York: Doubleday Books.
Jung, C. G. (1989) *Memories, Dreams, Reflections*. New York: Vintage Books.

3

THE BEGINNINGS OF THE ENTOURAGE

Emma Jung

> The Valkyries are also called Wish-Maidens; and now and then, one of them becomes, as Brunhilde did, the wife or lover of a great hero to whom she can give help and protection in battle.
>
> (Jung, E. 1985, p. 51)

This excerpt from the only written work to be completed by Emma Jung might well be a description of how she and others saw her role as wife to C. G. Jung. Throughout their marriage, which began in 1903, it was Emma who was seen by Jung as his "rock"; it was Emma who kept him grounded, particularly when he set out to plunge into his unconscious depths in the writing of the black books, then *The Red Book*. The love between them is not in question. She certainly stepped in to give help in at least one of Jung's crises, the break with Freud. In the increasingly formal letters, flying back and forth between the men in Zurich and Vienna, it was Emma's that had the voice of reason and that indicate she was the one who saw most clearly what was happening between her husband and his former mentor and father figure. Throughout her life and his it was she who tried to smooth his way, even financially, and to keep his life in equilibrium for him.

Very early in their married life, in letters soliciting advice from Freud (McGuire 1974, p. 440), Emma describes how she felt she had to speak stupidly in public to make sure no one would think she was trying to compete with her husband. However great her love – which appears to have been intense – it must have been galling for a woman of her intellectual gifts to stifle her thoughts and power in the presence of others, particularly the many women who had begun to arrive from all over the world to be analyzed and work with him. One wonders where such a mandate was born. Part of it came from the era and from the Swiss conception of those times of the role of woman, and some possibly from her own upbringing within that society. Especially since there were no signs that Jung was afraid of intellectual competition. Once she had decided on her role of wife to the great man and bearer of his children that came with astonishing regularity from the first year of their marriage, perhaps it was difficult to step into unknown and, until then, untraversed territory. There was also "the part of Jung's personal psychology that was affected by his experience of a split mother figure and a separate anima figure" (Douglas 2000, p. 36).

Once the children began to arrive, this split must have become more pronounced as Emma became a mother to three in rather rapid succession while they were living in their first apartment at the Burgholzli Clinic. In the beginning, she had aided Jung in his work, typing papers and such. With the advent of three children, this became impossible. It was at the Clinic in 1904 that Sabina Spielrein arrived as a patient. Gradually, Spielrein's treatment took more and more of Jung's time, though she was moved into an apartment in 1905 to begin her university work. Still Jung continued to treat her, and their relationship developed into something more personal. This was first just speculated upon, but was substantiated by the discovery of a cache of personal papers of Spielrein's in Geneva in the 1990s. Just when Emma became aware of the more personal nature of their relationship is not clear, but living in the Burgholzli with her growing family and in such proximity to her husband's work she must have become aware.

By 1911, when Emma had written the first of a series of letters to Freud, Toni Wolff had been on the scene for a year as an analysand of Jung's. She was to be yet another serious rival for Jung's affections, resulting in a triangle that lasted much of Emma's life. When Toni was invited to the Weimar Congress, Toni's mother asked that Jung and his wife Emma act as chaperones for her daughter. The Congress, held in Vienna, was the second of the International Psychoanalytic Association, which at its first Congress in Nuremberg had elected Jung as its first President. Toni must have been very proud to have an invitation offered by Jung to such a prestigious event. Sabina Spielrein was supposed to have attended, but withdrew at the last moment, possibly sensing a new rival on the scene. It was also at this point that Emma most possibly realized that her best chance of maintaining her marriage to Jung lay in not competing with Toni or Sabina or any other rumored women in C. G.'s life. She took refuge in her role, essential to Jung, of mother-container.

In *Memories, Dreams, Reflections*, Jung writes of the critical part of his life when he was wrestling with the unconscious contents that were welling up inside him and eventually became the substance of *The Red Book*.

> It was essential for me to have a normal life in the real world as a counterpoint to that strange inner world…. I have a wife and five children; I live at 228 Seestrasse in Kusnacht – these were actualities which made demands on me and proved to me again and again that I really existed, that I was not a blank page whirling about in the winds of the spirit like Nietzsche … a guarantee that I also had a normal existence.
>
> *(Jung 1989, p. 189)*

16 The beginnings of the entourage: Emma Jung

Emma realized his need for such normality in the face of what he was exploring and decided, with some ambivalence, to provide just that for him.

Emma Rauschenbach was the daughter of a wealthy industrialist from an old Swiss family. There are stories that Jung met her first when he was twenty-three and she was fourteen or fifteen, or perhaps sixteen years old, and told the friend who was with him at the time that she would one day be his wife. A pretty story, but things proved not to be that simple, as Emma refused him when he first asked her to marry him, then the second time, accepted. There are hints from varying sources that there was a rather stormy pre-nuptial relationship, with ups and downs.

While Emma was still a young girl, family tragedy struck when her father went blind from syphilis, causing him to become very bitter. Emma was prevented from going on to college. When Jung came to court her, his intellectual brilliance must have attracted her, and possibly like so many women of her time, she projected her own intellectual needs and abilities onto him.

Within a year of their marriage, she had her first child, and had four more children within the first eleven years of their marriage. Her letters to Freud began before she had her first child. And it was at that time that Toni Wolff came into the picture. In those post-Victorian days it was not unusual for another woman to appear, in a conventional marriage. What was unusual was that in time, this triangle was acknowledged by the three people concerned and they all attempted to live with it. Jung spent Wednesdays with Toni at her apartment, and she came to dinner at their house on Sundays. Later, the Jung children were to acknowledge this and their dislike of it, and cut all mention of Toni out of the autobiography of Jung. This arrangement was at least outwardly acceptable at the time, though in an interview with C. A. Meier, to whom both women came for therapy, he acknowledges there was much pain for both of them (Meier 1978).

This pain experienced by all three people was evident to all around them, and was guardedly expressed by sympathetic biographers of Jung. "Of course there were the most painful difficulties for everyone concerned, especially before a modus vivendi was reached" (Hannah 1981, p. 119). But "the dignity and willingness with which she [Toni Wolff] accepted this role and the apparent ease with which she ignored the world jealous of her special relationship with Jung, should not be allowed to disguise the staggering burdens it imposed upon her" (Van der Post 1977, p. 175).

Of course, perhaps Toni accepted it more easily than Emma because it gave her a special cachet to be privy to the thoughts and information coming from a man whom she and the others around him held in the highest regard. However, "they observed Toni repeatedly in the grip of great distress" (Van der Post 1977, p. 175). The author Laurens van der Post goes on to tell us how, at Bollingen Tower, constructed along the lines of the miniature stone house Jung built as a child, one stone is carved to Emma, referring to her as "the foundation of the house," while another is carved for Toni Wolff, "the fragrance of the house." One wonders whether Emma might have liked being the fragrance too. There is something very maternal about being the foundation. Whatever really went on in the hearts of those three will never really be known as all those letters are burned and the people have passed on.

But the best statement of Emma's feelings and her dilemma is contained in a letter to Freud dated November 24, 1911: "The women are naturally all in love with him.... Carl says I should no longer concentrate as before only on him and the children, but what on earth am I to do?" (McGuire 1974, p. 467).

The letter poses a question that would be a difficult to answer, even in these more liberated days, for a woman who had hitherto devoted her energies to a growing family and finds herself no longer the chief object of her husband's attentions. And considering how much more restrictive were women's roles at that time, and in Switzerland, so much more confusing for the woman. Jung seemed at times to formulate things in such a way that he freed himself and his conscience, while still appearing liberal for the era.

Emma turned to analytical work as she began to have more time to herself.

> Although Jung first psychoanalyzed Emma Jung, then involved her in analytical work and encouraged her to develop her own intellectual interests, he felt she existed as his satellite. She was in his eyes first and foremost contained within their marriage as his wife and mother of their five children.
> *(Douglas 2000, p. 36)*

Nowadays we are staggered at the idea of Jung analyzing his own wife. However, it is good to remember that in the early days of psychiatry there was practically no formulation or rules about transference and the boundaries were fluid to say the least. It is almost (but not quite) amusing to read in one of Jung's letters to Freud that he writes of his wife being pregnant again and complains that her sessions of analysis with him are marred by a number of her "jealous scenes" (Fordham 1979).

One of Emma's first patients, who was receiving analysis from Jung, was sent to her by Jung because she dreamed that Emma had something for her. This was the beginning of a pattern that continued throughout many years among Jung, Toni, and Emma; many people had analysis with at least two of them.

People who knew Emma in those years have said she seemed like a fulfilled woman who enjoyed her career and brooked no nonsense from Jung. Since these observations were made from outside the triangle there is no way to know how accurate they are. Many apparently "happy" marriages break up every day.

According to at least one observer, Emma had a sense of humor when dealing with her husband and was never in awe of him. Once, at dinner, someone asked why he did not deal with children. He replied that they did not interest him as they didn't have much symbolic material. Emma commented, "Oh, Carl! No one interests you who doesn't have much symbolic material" (Serrano 1988, p. 58). There were many occasions when she deflated him if he appeared to her to become too full of hubris. According to Dr. Michael Fordham, she often aimed a well-placed kick under the table at Jung when he made some outrageous or pompous remark.

She did not embark on her large work on the Grail until after her children were well on their way to growing up. However, her interest in the subject dated from her early years. It has been suggested it might have begun during a trip to Paris before she married, where she was introduced to Chretien de Troyes' *Romance of the Round Table*. Another source says that an ancestor of hers failed on his quest and she felt a need to explore the myth for that reason. Whatever the impetus, her interest grew and she began reading and researching material and collected a small mountain of notes on the subject of the Grail. She was often asked to speak on it at the Psychological Club. When Jung took a trip to England in April 1939, Emma went along, and when his work there was done, she asked that they take a trip to the West Country, to Glastonbury, to explore more of the Arthurian territory.

Jung, of course, had his own interest in the Grail legends. He had read at age fifteen of the Knights of the Round Table, and on his trip to India in 1937–1938 he had a dream that influenced the development of his work. He speaks of the incongruity of having such a dream in India, but realized its meaning for him: "[I]t seemed quite natural to me that the dream should conjure up the world of the Knights of the Grail and their quest – for that was, in the deepest sense, my own world" (Jung 1989, p. 165). As one Jungian analyst puts it, "Jung came to consider the myth of the Grail as a myth of Western man and in this sense, also his myth" (Guerra 2014, p. 67). This same analyst also remarks on one of the first visions in *The Red Book*, where Jung "saw a red point coming near, a horseman, the Red One" (Guerra 2014, p. 67). He likens it to the Red Knight encountered by Parsifal in his quest. Like Parsifal, Jung conquers the Red One and takes his armor.

Later, Jung was to write:

> It was as though the dream was asking me, "What are you doing in India? Rather seek for yourself and your fellows the healing vessel, the servator mundi, which you urgently need. For your state is perilous; you are all in danger of destroying all that centuries have built up."
>
> *(Jung 1989, p. 281)*

And what, one wonders, would Jung think of the world now?

Emma began to gather her notes to start writing a book, but it was never finished before she died. Jung asked Marie-Louise von Franz to complete the work, which she did (von Franz 1970). Several people to whom I spoke, and who had seen fragments of Emma's work on the Grail, felt her writing about it superior to what von Franz finally published. I was unable to find any existing notes of the lectures Emma Jung gave to the Psychological Club using her own material, to my regret. And the book, possibly more greatly influenced by von Franz than Emma, stresses the quest for the Grail as a man's journey. However, as I can personally testify, it is very much a human quest, not specific to any one gender. As Jessie L. Weston, whose books on the subject are in the bibliography of *The Grail Legends*, writes, "The Grail Story is not … the product of imagination, literary or popular. At its root lies the record, more or less distorted, of an ancient Ritual, having for its ultimate object the initiation into the secret of Life, physical and spiritual" (Weston 1957, back cover).

Emma's first work was published in 1931, twenty-seven years into the Jungs' marriage. This was on the concept of the animus, based on a lecture she gave at the Zurich Psychological Club. "Emma Jung was the first to strongly rework, elaborate, and expand on C. G. Jung's description of the animus … appearing in a paper 'On the Nature of the Animus'" (Douglas 2000, p. 152). Modern feminists have pointed to this paper as portraying "a positive picture of a woman achieving emotional and intellectual independence … she drew attention to the problems of women in a society that refuses to support their inner development" (Rowland 2002, p. 51). This was published, together with another paper on the anima, which adheres more closely and unquestioningly to Jung's doctrine.

Many men find it expedient after years of marriage to relate to their wives mainly as mother to their children, and in some way to become children to their wives. Many times the wife has become so caught up in the rigors of caring for the home and children that she is not aware of the emotional defection of her husband until it is too late. However, we must assume that Emma, being as intelligent and psychologically fine-tuned as she was, certainly was aware. How could she not be, given first the affair with Spielrein, then the long relationship with Toni? Jung is reported to have said to Miguel Serrano that "in my long psychiatric experience, I never came across a marriage that was entirely self-sufficient … ideally the man should contain the woman and remain outside her" (Down 1988, p. 116). Jung had told Freud he was suffering from the "nuptial complex" and said finally, "The prerequisite for a good marriage it seems to me is the license to be unfaithful" (Serrano 1988, p. 58). "I think the French have found the solution in the Number Three. Frequently this number occurs in magic marriages" (Brome 2001, p. 248). This seems to be true in the Jungs' marriage: Number Three coming in the person of Toni Wolff.

Emma's death in 1955 shook the foundation of Jung's life, and he never totally recovered from it. In old age, he had turned to his wife more and more. And in a later interview, when asked if he believed in life after death, he said he "knew" there was life after death, recounting a dream he had of seeing his wife after her death on a stage, and running to get to her, but finding an abyss where the orchestra pit should be. Life and death separated thus. Ruth Bailey, who lived in as caretaker in Jung's old age, said that Toni had become somewhat of a burden in his older years and that Emma's death affected him more profoundly than Toni's had, a few years before (Brome 2001). He obviously felt that with Emma's passing, the "help and protection in battle" had been withdrawn, never to be replaced.

References

Brome, Vincent (2001) *Jung: Man and Myth*. Looe, UK: House of Stratus.
Douglas, Claire (2000) *The Woman in the Mirror: Analytical Psychology and the Feminine*. Lincoln, Nebraska: iUniverse. First published Boston: Sigo Press, 1990.
Down, L. (1988) *Freud and Jung: Years of Friendship, Years of Loss*. New York: Scribner.
Fordham, Michael (January 1979) Author's interview.

Guerra, Maria Helena Mandarcaru (2014) *The Love Drama of C. G. Jung as Revealed in His Life and in His Red Book*. Montreal: Inner City Books.
Hannah, Barbara (1981) *Jung: His Life and Work*. Boston: Shambhala Publications.
Jung, C. G. (1989) *Memories, Dreams, Reflections*. New York: Vintage Books.
Jung, Emma (1985) *Anima and Animus*. Dallas, Texas: Spring Publications.
McGuire, William, ed. (1974) *The Freud–Jung Letters*. Princeton, New Jersey: Princeton University Press.
Meier, C. A. (May 1978) Author's interview.
Rowland, Susan (2002) *Jung: A Feminist Revision*. Cambridge: Polity Press.
Serrano, Miguel (1988) *C. G. Jung and Hermann Hesse: A Record of Two Friendships*. New York: Schocken.
Van der Post, Sir Laurens (1977) *Jung and the Story of Our Time*. New York: Vintage Books.
Von Franz, Marie-Louise (1970) *The Grail Legend*. With Emma Jung. New York: Putnam's Sons/C. G. Jung Foundation.
Weston, Jessie L. (1957) *From Ritual to Romance*. New York: Doubleday Anchor Books.

4

SIEGFRIED'S MATE

Sabina Spielrein

As more and more of Jung's innermost work comes out and is examined, particularly with the 2009 publication of *The Red Book*, his own psychological complexity is apparent. He began to be an unlikely hero of American pop culture beginning in the late 1960s, ten years after his death, as evidenced in one way by the influx of young American students coming to study at the C. G. Jung Institute in Zurich (as I mention in Chapter 19, my memoir of my year at that Institute).

This trend of popularity, in the counter-culture particularly, continues. Recently Jung, Freud, and Sabina Spielrein became the unlikely subjects of a Hollywood film, with all the attendant exaggerations and dramatic license, and a small ration of books. Yet the importance of Spielrein to an understanding of Jung's work, and indeed the development of analytical psychology, merits much more study and there are subtleties that have yet to be examined, despite the spate of interest in her in the last few years. Ignore the importance of Spielrein in the psychological development of Jung and his work at your peril.

It is important therefore to delve into the life and work of this woman, who was herself so complex, though I shall not give her background in great detail as that has been done in other books recently published (Carotenuto 1982; Covington and Wharton 2003; Kerr 1998; Launer 2011).

Sabina Spielrein was the oldest child of four, and only daughter of a prosperous, well-educated Russian Jewish family who had risen from a traditional Orthodox Jewish background to become part of the wealthy middle class. Her maternal grandfather was a well-known and respected rabbi, who nonetheless encouraged his daughter to go to a Christian school to study science and become a dentist. He was equally encouraging of his granddaughter, Sabina. She was not only a good student, but spoke Russian, Polish, German, and French. Additionally, she chose to study Hebrew so she could read the Bible in its original form. Her family moved in an intellectual milieu in their native Rostov-on-Don on the Black Sea, and in addition traveled widely in Europe.

There are indications, however, that both parents provided a less-than-healthy psychological atmosphere for the children. There are allegations of child abuse concerning her father. All of Sabina's younger brothers had a variety of nervous disorders. But it was Sabina who, in 1904, began to show symptoms of an increasingly worrisome kind. Eventually, her mother and her mother's brother took her to Switzerland to a mental hospital, where she stayed for a time, but without success. After a couple more unsuccessful tries at other institutions, she came to the Burgholzli Clinic in Zurich, where she would eventually find a cure. She was diagnosed as a hysteric, a not uncommon diagnosis for troubled young women at a time when women were supposed to be paragons of virtue, and every household had smelling salts ready for them, in case their fragile constitutions were exposed to anything out of the ordinary. This was particularly true of upper-class women. There were many forbidden topics, among them anything to do with sexuality or other bodily functions. This led, of course, to a good deal of repression, and when women found they were unable to get the attention and care they needed in any other way, hysterical outbursts and extreme agitation achieved it. It was there in the Burgholzli Clinic that Spielrein's care was given over to a young psychiatrist, Dr. C. G. Jung, only twenty-nine years old himself. The head of the hospital, Dr. Eugen Bleuler, suggested to Jung that she be treated in the method of a new pioneer in the field, Dr. Sigmund Freud of Vienna, then known as the "talking cure." Jung had read much of Freud's work, so he enthusiastically took on his first patient, Sabina Spielrein, to be treated in the new method. Jung at this time was a handsome young man, full of life and energy, and at the very beginning of what would become the working out of a life-changing method for the healing of souls. With Spielrein, he used Freud's method of psychoanalysis, though he had no formal training in it. He saw her once a day, talking with her for at least an hour and sometimes up to three hours. She may have been one of the first patients upon whom he used his own method of word association to reveal the complexes within her, which were a key to her mental instability.

She started out her stay with the most hysterical outbursts, taunting the nurses and staff by her threatened suicides, and pulling off childish pranks to annoy them and get further attention. Gradually, under Jung's care, she began to calm down. She became rational and calm enough to eventually begin helping him in his research and assisting him in his work. However, as she recovered, Jung made a note that she was becoming more sensuous in her response to him, a not unusual behavior in transference between a patient and her analyst. After a relatively short stay of approximately ten months, she was considered healed and guided to the University of Zurich to study medicine as she had originally intended. However, she did continue to see Jung as her analyst, and there are indications that her feelings had indeed escalated into amorous ones. This is especially noticeable in her journal entries from after June 1905 when she was discharged to go to medical school, and in letters home to her mother. The letters, however, might be seen also to be provocations to worry her mother. She did, however, excel in her studies and seemed to be settling down into her new life as a serious student. She began to send letters to Jung in 1906, which was the year in which Jung began his correspondence with Freud.

Though she did not remain in Jung's circle, which was then in its earliest stages, for more than a very few of the early years of his practice, Sabina Spielrein must certainly be included among the Valkyries in his life. In fact, it might be claimed that she was the original one, since she envisioned him in her personal psychology as Siegfried and herself as Brunhilde, and told him so. As time went on, they shared together what Jung had interpreted in her dreams, although there are indications she did not always agree with his interpretations. In them was the idea of her giving him a son, also to be called Siegfried. In her journals, there are indications she thought the child, Siegfried, actually symbolically referred to the "great work" she was destined to do. In writing of her work a few years later on the concept of death and sexuality, one author states:

> In the case of Sabina Spielrein, her "eroticised" phantasy of mutual death is evident in her transference to Jung, most notably in the comparison Spielrein makes between herself and Jung and Wagner's Brünnhilde and Siegfried in *The Ring of the Nibelung*.
>
> *(Covington 2003, p. 12)*

During Sabina's time at the University of Zurich, *Siegfried* was performed in the city, and while it is unknown whether Jung attended, Spielrein as a great lover of music, and particularly what she termed "Wagner's psychological music," most certainly would have. This performance might well have been the genesis of her fantasy. In 1909, she wrote, in the draft of a letter, "It was Wagner who planted the demon in my soul with such terrifying clarity. I shall omit the metaphors, since you might laugh at the extravagance of my emotion" (Kerr 1998).

In recent books written about the Spielrein–Jung affair, much speculation has taken place about whether it was actually physically consummated, or whether the "poetry," which Spielrein alludes to in her journals, was simply no more than what we would today call heavy petting. Actually, she seems to have found the term "poetry" in her reading of a contemporary writer on psychology, August Forel, in his 1905 work, *The Sexual Question*. She used his metaphor of "poetry" to describe amorous intoxication (Kerr 1998). Many believe there really was sexual intercourse because of the intensity of both of them in their letters to one another.

In Jung and Spielrein's case, one of the major reasons for it not going "all the way" would undoubtedly be the fear of pregnancy, which would have ruined her, and perhaps also Jung's marriage. In one letter to her mother, most probably written in late 1908, she writes, "So far we have remained at the level of poetry that is not dangerous, and we shall remain at that level, perhaps until the time I will become a doctor, unless circumstances alter" (Lothene 2003). Although in her journals that have survived, she writes often of the fact that she would not really want to be the cause of his leaving his wife and children, and is very aware of the damage it would do to her plans for a career and future if she had a child out of wedlock, the last may indicate wistful thinking about him leaving them. But the fire and intensity was there, and in her journal entry of June 22, 1912, she writes, "No ashes, no coal can burn with such glow/as a secretive love/of which no one must know" (Covington 2003, p. 1). And perhaps the very intensity owed itself, in part, to the secrecy.

That Jung himself was ensnared with the fantasy of Siegfried and Brunhilde, is now evident, I believe, in entries in *The Red Book*, although on his part it seems largely unconscious. Of course, he might have chosen that road, as possibly indicated in a footnote in the volume just below where he has written his own fantasy, based on a dream he had. The fantasy reads:

> Oh that Siegfried, blond and blue-eyed, the German hero, had to fall by my hand, the most loyal and courageous! He had everything in himself that I treasured as the greater and beautiful: he was my power, my boldness, my pride. I would have gone under in the same battle, and so only assassination was left to me. If I wanted to go on living, it could be only by trickery and cunning.

At the bottom of the same page, the editor quotes from a talk Jung gave at a 1925 seminar.

> Siegfried was not an especially sympathetic figure to me, and *I don't know why my unconscious got engrossed in him* [author's italics]. Wagner's Siegfried, especially, is exaggeratedly extraverted and at times actually ridiculous. I never liked him. Nevertheless the dream showed him to be my hero. I could not understand the strong emotion I had with the dream.
>
> (Jung 2009, p. 242, n. 115)

The dream had taken place in December of 1913, not too long after the break-up with Sabina. In enlarging on the dream, he spoke of the need to kill the heroic ego. However, he must have known, as anyone working with dreams and imagery knows, that there are many layers and levels of meaning to such material.

Was it perhaps the leftover emotion that he had about his affair with Spielrein? And had he actually forgotten the time and place where Siegfried had entered his unconscious in a personal way? One would not expect him to reveal as much publicly; however, it seems a bit disingenuous for him to speak of being so very puzzled at this archetypal hero in his unconscious. And is it the elder Siegfried whom he has killed, or the son that he had felt Spielrein had dreams of during their relationship? Perhaps both, as he had written in a letter to her in December of 1908:

> Will you forgive me for being as I am? Forgetting my duties as a doctor toward you? Will you understand that I am one of the weakest human beings? … It is my misfortune that I cannot live without the joy of love, of tempestuous, ever-changing love in my life.… When love for a woman awakens within me, the first thing I feel is regret, pity for the poor woman who dreams of eternal faithfulness and other impossibilities, and is destined for a painful awakening out of all these dreams.
>
> (Wharton 2001)

We must remember that the affair itself, whatever lengths at which it was expressed, took place at the very beginnings of the theory of psychoanalysis as laid out by Sigmund Freud. And once Jung had written to Freud of the consequences of the affair, though not speaking of his obvious part in it, Freud at once responded in a letter, the first of many to Jung.

> I myself have never been taken in so badly, but I have come very close to it a number of times and had a narrow escape.... They help us to develop a thick skin we need and to dominate "countertransference," which is after all a permanent problem for us.
>
> *(McGuire 1974, p. 231)*

"This is the first time the expression 'countertransference', which will later become a scientific term, appears in psychoanalytic literature" (McGuire 1974).

It was in 1911 that the famous Weimar Congress was held, and the often-reproduced picture of those attending is shown. It is in the first row that we see and know of Toni Wolff, of whom Jung wrote to Freud, that she was his "new discovery" and had an "excellent feeling for religion and philosophy." Spielrein, who was also to attend, is conspicuous by her absence, though Emma Jung is there.

It seems that Spielrein, more than likely learning of Jung's latest disciple and patient, Toni Wolff, and his deepening interest in her, declined at the last moment to attend. In a letter, Jung takes her to task for this in a heavy-handed manner.

> I can see your situation clearly. I can hardly think that there is anything organically wrong with your foot [Spielrein had used 'foot pain' as her excuse for not attending], for the psychological situation is too powerfully and traumatically significant. Something in you was searching for a reason not to go to Weimar. In other words, you wanted to come with a certain phantasy/wish that you had to repress. You ought to have come in spite of that, however, for life demands sacrifices and self-denial.
>
> *(Wharton 2001)*

Though obviously not from Jung himself.

It was around this time, and after, that Jung began to develop his concept of the archetypes of the anima and animus. And a modern Jungian analyst has written, "Jung's anima problem (which was enormous – at the time of these imaginations, he had broken with Freud in a rage and was plunged into a marital crisis as well, having decided to accept his former patient Toni Wolff as a lover)" (Beebe 2005). It was also at this time, after the Weimar Congress, that he persuaded Emma to accept Toni into their family life. He had evidently tried something similar earlier, with Spielrein, but she was beyond the pale for Emma. An entry in Spielrein's journal states that "True, he wanted to introduce me in his house, make me his wife's friend, but understandably, his wife wanted no part of this business" (Carotenuto 1982). If one looks closely at Toni's picture at Weimar, and pictures of Spielrein, there are obvious similarities in type. Both are dark-haired, dark-eyed and intense, with a "foreign" look about them. As had Jung's earliest anima image, the maid who comforted him as a child in his mother's absence. But Toni had the advantage of being Swiss, from a prominent family. And as Sabina wrote in her journal, "He told me he would never marry me because he is a great philistine and needs the typical Swiss style" (Carotenuto 1982). Toni had this "Swiss style" and evidently, though it pained her, Emma was able to accept Toni because of this, rather than the Russian-Jewish Spielrein, who was "foreign."

The source of the anima in a man most often has to do with his relationship to his mother and the sort of mother she was. This was as true of Jung as it is of all the men in Jungian analysis. Jung was quite aware of this, as we see in several passages in his autobiography, *Memories, Dreams, Reflections*. In one of the earliest mentions, he writes, "Dim intimations of trouble in my parents' marriage hovered around me.... My mother spent several months in a hospital in Basel and presumably her illness had something to do with the difficulty in the marriage" (Beebe 2005). There has been much speculation as to just what this illness was. However, in Spielrein's journals she has one entry that seemingly solves the mystery. "It was predestined he would love me. He is like a father to me – and I am rather like a mother. His mother became ill with hysteria when he was two years old. He fell in love with me … a hysteric!" (Launer 2011).

Meanwhile, Spielrein's studies were coming along well. Her desire to become a psychiatrist and do for others what she had felt Jung's treatment had done for her was becoming paramount in her mind. In November 1911, she presented at the Vienna Psychoanalytical Society her paper, "Destruction as the Cause of Coming Into Being." It was a work which would influence both Jung and Freud, and which each would acknowledge publicly later, though possibly not as strongly as they might have. The paper states:

> One feels the enemy inside oneself, in one's glowing love, which forces one, with iron necessity, to do what one doesn't want to do: one feels the end, the fleetingness, from which one vainly tries to flee to distances unknown. "Is that all?" one wants to ask. "Is this the climax, and nothing beyond?"
>
> *(Launer 2011)*

According to John Launer:

> The key part of her paper now follows … "Biological Facts." These few short paragraphs contain the essence of Spielrein's argument. They are entirely unlike anything written by Freud, Jung, or other contemporary writers on sex like Krafft-Ebing or Havelock Ellis. Indeed there appears to be nothing like them in the psychological literature for almost another century.
>
> *(Launer 2011)*

Much later, in the last several years he took patients, Jung would insist they have their astrological charts done first as he believed that in seeing the chart, he could "cut to the chase" as it were, the chart providing indications of where the complexes might lie. If we follow that idea, for the purposes of understanding these complicated relationships further, it seems Jung missed out by not incorporating astrology earlier. If he had, he might have seen that, for instance, Spielrein, born on November 7, 1885, was a triple Scorpio. That is, she had her Sun, Moon, and Mercury in that constellation. Simply put, her essential nature was Scorpio, her emotional nature was Scorpio, and her thinking function, too. This becomes even more interesting when we see the direction her psychological studies took, as evidenced by the paper quoted above. For the sign of Scorpio is indelibly intertwined with sex, death, and regeneration. And sexuality of a specific sort: "The urge of the individual to merge in absolute union with other individuals in order to constitute together a greater organic whole" (Wright 1987). And then, there is Jung's own chart, as interpreted by one of the great astrologers of the twentieth century, Dane Rudhyar:

> Jung's chart shows at once how difficult it would be for ordinary bio-social structures of themselves to hold in check his unusually aroused life energies! ... Bio-psychic energy is restless and explosive in Jung's being and could easily lead to emotional explosions of a peculiar overwhelming of the conscious by the unconscious.
>
> *(Rudhyar 1976)*

Jung and Spielrein's most intense period of relationship seems to have peaked between 1908 and 1911. But it was in 1912 that she submitted her paper, "Destruction as the Cause of Coming into Being," to Jung, as editor of the *Yearbook* of the psychoanalytical movement. She wrote to him that this is "the product of our love, the project which is our little son, Siegfried" (Launer 2011). In reply she received a cold, formal letter. But the paper was published.

A few months afterward, in June 1912, she married a hitherto unmentioned Dr. Paul Scheftel, simply stating in her journal the fact, with one sentence added: "To be continued" (Launer 2011). She moved to Berlin shortly after this marriage and a year later gave birth to her daughter Renata. Shortly before the First World War broke out, she moved to Geneva, where she did some clinical work and supervision, had Jean Piaget as a private patient, and did some theatre reviews for the *Journal de Genève*. It was at the Psychological Institute in Geneva that she deposited journals, letters, and other memorabilia in their archives. It is to the discovery of these in 1977 that we owe most of what we know of Spielrein, who might otherwise have remained only a footnote in the history of psychology.

In 1923 she returned to Russia for various reasons, one of which was to further the aims of her research and belief in Freudian psychology. Unfortunately, Russia's Institute was abolished on political grounds, followed in 1930 by the abolition of the Russian Psychoanalytical Society. The iron fist of Stalin was beginning to make itself felt. Beginning in 1935, her three brothers and her father were systematically imprisoned, then killed by the regime. Her husband died in 1938, and so she shared with his mistress the responsibility of the child the mistress had had by him, as well as Spielrein's own two daughters. She was urged to leave Rostov, where she had gone to be with her husband and his family, but chose to remain. In 1942, she and her two daughters were executed by the Nazis, who had invaded Rostov. Some reports say the execution took place in a ravine outside of town, others say a great number of Jews were herded into the synagogue and murdered there.

A bronze plaque in the Venice ghetto reads, "their only grave is in our memories."

But there is another "grave" for Spielrein, though significantly in it she still remains nameless.

> [L]eft behind in the Bollingen retreat is a symbolic record, executed in stone.... Among these is a stone triptych on the subject of "anima." The initial panel shows a bear bending down, its nose nudging a ball along in front of it. The inscription reads, "Russia gets the ball rolling." It is a sad last testament to Spielrein that even in a stone monument in her honor she could not be named.
>
> *(Kerr 1998, p. 507)*

References

Beebe, John (2005) *Integrity in Depth*. Dallas: Texas A&M University Press.

Carotenuto, Aldo (1982) *A Secret Symmetry*. New York: Pantheon.

Covington, Julie (2003) "Introduction." In *Sabina Spielrein: Forgotten Pioneer of Psychoanalysis*, Coline Covington and Barbara Wharton, eds. Hove: Brunner-Routledge, pp. 1–14.

Covington, Coline and Wharton, Barbara, eds. (2003) *Sabina Spielrein: Forgotten Pioneer of Psychoanalysis*. Hove: Brunner-Routledge.

Jung, C. G. (2009) *The Red Book: The Reader's Edition*, ed. Sonu Shamdasani. New York: W. W. Norton.

Kerr, John (1998) *A Most Dangerous Method: The Story of Jung, Freud, and Sabina Spielrein*. New York: Alfred Knopf.

Launer, John (2011) *Sex vs. Survival: The Story of Sabina Spielrein: Her Life, Her Ideas, Her Genius*. Morrisville, North Carolina: Lulu Press.

Lothene, Zoe, trans. (2003) "Tender Love and Transference: Unpublished Letters of C. G. Jung and Sabina Spielrein." In *Sabina Spielrein: Forgotten Pioneer of Psychoanalysis*, Coline Covington and Barbara Wharton, eds. Hove: Brunner-Routledge, pp. 191–226.

McGuire, William, ed. (1974) *The Freud–Jung Letters*. Princeton, New Jersey: Princeton University Press.

Rudhyar, Dane (1976) *Astrology and the Modern Psyche*. Sebastopol, California: CRCS.

Wharton, Barbara, trans. (2001) "Letters of C. G. Jung to Sabina Spielrein." *Journal of Analytical Psychology* 46(1): 173–199.

Wright, Paul (1987) *The Literary Zodiac*. Edinburgh: Anodyne Publishers.

5
THE FRAGRANCE
Toni Wolff

Sabina Spielrein was not quite out of the picture when Fate stepped in and delivered Toni Wolff into analysis with Jung. Fate, in the form of Frau Wolff, Toni's mother, who had tried several other doctors to cure her daughter, who had had a nervous breakdown at the death of her father.

Antonia Wolff was born in 1888, thirteen years after Jung. She was, like him, a native-born Swiss. Her father, whom she adored, was an aristocrat and a successful businessman, a combination much admired in Switzerland. He was twenty years older than his wife. He had an affinity with Japan, where he often traveled, and there were even rumors he had Japanese blood, which gave him his "foreign" good looks. Toni, too, had something of the exotic in her dark, brooding beauty – something un-Swiss. Something reminiscent of the maid in young Carl's childhood, and the dark good looks of the Russian Sabina. Someone once described Toni as a black pearl, and Jung agreed with this description around the time she came into treatment with him in 1910 (Donn 1988, p. 26).

Jung's professional reputation was just beginning to spread and several of Jung's associates have speculated that Toni Wolff was the case referred to as Jung's one cure of schizophrenia. If this is true, it might be that his own subsequent "descent into the unconscious" had more than a little to do with the contamination that can take place within an analyst when working with a schizophrenic patient. This is said to occur when a specific illness being treated meets the unconscious working out of similar problems in the analyst.

At this time, Toni was a dark, intense-looking young woman who was just beginning to project the rather forbidding persona she may have further developed to protect her very vulnerable nature, which had been placed in a trying situation. "Her personal dislike of women may have been partly due to her own personality combined with her experience in Zurich … [she] was also in the ambiguous and vulnerable social position of being Jung's publicly acknowledged mistress" (Douglas 2000, p. 115).

Even in the later 1970s when I was interviewing the surviving Jungian women who were contemporaries, Wolff's name either evoked complete silence or a guarded appreciation of her role as Jung's assistant. At no time did I hear the word "mistress" from anyone, yet quite simply, or not so simply, that was her role. She became his collaborator and did some independent work on his psychology. The fact remains that her involvement with Jung, at least in the beginning, was as the "other woman" in a whispered, but much discussed, triangle. This triangle of Jung, Emma, and Toni has been alternately praised for its openness (Emma was aware of the relationship, perhaps from the start), and deplored for the pain it inflicted on both women. More rarely, the question is asked why Jung insisted on such a relationship continuing in view of the obvious pain it caused his wife. The fact remains that he did. Toni has been referred to as Jung's *femme inspiratrice*, *soror mystica*, or anima, which translate as inspiring woman, or muse, mystical sister as in the alchemical opuses, and soul. They all sound quite high-flown and more like the official titles reigning monarchs bestow on their lovers, or terms poets might use to describe important relationships with women, usually mistresses, seldom wives. To his credit, there is no indication that Jung himself used any of them. They imply a transcendence of the physical realm into the spiritual. This was certainly the case with Jung and Toni Wolff, who was not only analyzed by, but also analyzed her mentor. The terms were used by his followers, perhaps to avoid the negative publicity that would have emerged if Jung had been known to have a mistress. Sounding rather arch at best and kittenish at worst, they continue to have been used in biographies of Jung until recently. In the course of my interviews, I was often told his relationship with Toni was "different." It did not seem to occur to those who employed these terms and explanations that they were no longer necessary. The revelation simply serves to show that Jung was as human as many before him and since.

This, then, was the young woman who appeared in Jung's life during a critical phase – in astrology, called the Uranian transit – approaching middle age. Jung was thirty-five and had already been married for seven years. Within a year of beginning her analysis, Toni was invited by Jung to the congress at Weimar, along with his wife. Jung had written a letter beforehand to Freud, describing "Fraulein Antonia Wolff, a remarkable intellect with an excellent feeling for religion and philosophy" (McGuire 1974, p. 440). She appears in the much-published picture taken at Weimar in 1911, discreetly separated from Jung and Emma by another woman. She appears wide-eyed, intense, and questioning.

By 1911, Emma needed an analytical confidant and began to correspond with Freud, discussing the strains on her marriage. Jung was not aware of this correspondence until it ended. Among her numerous complaints were the many women who gathered around her husband, "while with the men I am constantly cordoned off as the wife of the father or friend" (McGuire 1974, p. 440). Any guessing as to the date when the relationship between Jung and Toni began slipping beyond that of doctor–patient is futile. It is as good a guess as any that it was most probably after the break with Freud was final. This also coincided with Jung's descent into the unconscious, the first of his visions and the early beginnings of *The Red Book*. It also marked the end of Toni's therapy, which Jung once told a friend had lasted three years. After the break with Freud, Jung felt cast adrift and friendless. He felt also he was putting his chosen profession in jeopardy, and, psychologically speaking, was committing patricide. (Freud had once interpreted one of Jung's dreams to mean that Jung had an unconscious desire to kill him.) Jung was beginning one of the most tortuous periods of his life, and one he felt absolutely to be the basis of his psychology later. His fantasies took on a peculiar half-life of their own, which made him fear for his sanity. In fact, he states in his autobiography that "in the drawer of my night table lay a loaded revolver and I became frightened" (Hannah 1976, p. 180). This was so that if he felt he was being taken over by his own psychological material, he could take his life and spare his family.

One of the first fantasies that appeared to him, as I've written in the Introduction, was a vision of the seemingly ill-assorted couple of Salome and Elijah, the young woman and the old prophet. Jung recorded how he questioned the phantom figure as to the appropriateness of the pairing. To this the old man replied, "they had been together throughout all of eternity." Perhaps this was his psyche's way of giving meaning to the troubling relationship that was developing with Toni. Again, in *Memories, Dreams, Reflections* there is no mention of Toni Wolff. This was due to his children and grandchildren demanding of Aniela Jaffé, who was taking notes and dictation from Jung for what was to be his last book, that all mention of Wolff be expunged. In some Jungian circles it is wondered aloud just how much of that book came from Jung.

> Before he died, Jung realized Jaffé had made changes to his original remarks that she was, in his coinage, "auntifying" (Tantifizierung, auntification) is how he expressed it, his earthy and often outspoken language in order to make it more acceptable to conventional readers.
>
> *(Lachman 2010, p. 228, n. 2)*

Just how he would have felt about having Toni Wolff completely removed from it, we can only imagine.

For it was to Toni that he turned as he began his descent into the dark, largely unexplored realms of the unconscious. Emma had her hands full with several children and the mechanics of what contemporaries have described as a beautifully run household. She was the rock, after all, the foundation, and it was possible Jung did not want her to accompany him in this dangerous undertaking for fear he might infect her. Emma was to say, many years later after Toni died, "I shall always be grateful to her for doing for my husband what I or anyone else could not have done at a most critical time" (Van der Post 1977, p. 177).

Just what she did we can only guess from similar experiences in Jungian analysis. In the first place she must have done a great deal of listening. And she would have had to be non-judgmental in attitude. In essence, she had to become his analyst.

When one is describing the dreams and fantasies which arise in archaic, peculiar, and often seemingly ridiculous form, it is important the listener does not interpret, as often this will interrupt the natural flow of images. The material of fantasy is so close to the wanderings of the mind in schizophrenic breaks as to be almost indistinguishable. This occurs when the material from the unconscious comes into the consciousness in the form of images and visions, which are uncontrolled. It is the source of the psychiatric term "acute schizophrenia," which is much more easily treated than paranoid schizophrenia. There must not be any overt or even subliminal message to the person experiencing them that the symbols are "crazy" or "stupid," for that is often just what that person fears. By his own admission, Jung feared this. The images must be treated as "real" but not worried in the manner in which a cat worries a mouse. Toni, with her poet's sensibilities, was most likely to take these images and treat them as metaphors, and research them in the literature of the then young sciences of anthropology and folklore. When a dream symbol seems particularly strange or worrisome, this is sometimes the best medicine – to find the symbol as it connects to mythologies.

With Toni both physically and emotionally so close, able to devote her time to him in a way which a woman with a household to run and five children to raise could not, there must have also been a degree of ambivalence. It is interesting to speculate that the severity of his struggle, which she helped to ease, might have been intensified by the complications such a relationship brought to his life. There is no doubt that he loved Emma and felt her central to his life, and so it is hardly likely he would have started such an intense relationship as that with Toni without inner turmoil.

Whatever the agonies that Jung suffered, the complications were worse for Toni. For, while in England and a few other European countries there has always been a niche for the unmarried woman, albeit a rather narrow one, no such niche appears to have existed in Swiss culture. There was the added difficulty of loving a prominent married man. One begins to see what were the stresses for her. "A friend who knew Toni well said of Jung, 'One can say he was a big spoon – he drank her soul.'" One of her former patients has written that an American friend of hers who was in Zurich in the early 1920s and 1930s said of Toni's equivocal position, "My God, she was courageous. She just MADE them accept it" (Wheelwright, Jane 1977).

Something that also aided in the acceptance of the relationship was that quality of Toni's which many have mentioned: her spinsterish, forbidding air, which as previously discussed was built as a bulwark against comment. Someone in the inner circle remarked, "Toni was all spirit. It was almost as if she HAD no body" (Donn 1988, p. 178). Perhaps this kept enough people from being certain about the exact nature of their relationship. Dr. Jolande Jacobi, another of the Jungian women, maintained that Jung was undersexed, but this is generally thought to be jealousy on her part. But there were still Jungians from that time who wondered out loud if anything physical between Jung and Toni ever took place. In view of the pain of both Emma and Toni this view seems hardly worthy of consideration.

Toni became Jung's assistant and her duties seem to have been mainly with research into the imagery emerging from his unconscious, which he later was to call the *Prima Materia* for all his future thought and work. Many of the women around him who became assistants in the following years also performed these tasks for him. In addition, she often accompanied him on his increasingly frequent trips abroad, along with Emma. During one of these trips to the Tavistock lectures in England, Toni brought such a number of hat boxes that an observer was sure she had a hat for every day of the visit. She dressed like a Parisienne in "well-cut dresses, her hair always beautifully done, waved back from her forehead. Very elegant" (Donn 1988, p. 178).

On another trip, to the Ravenna mosaics, Jung and Toni had an experience that can only be described as a joint vision, showing how strong was the psychic link between them. As they went into the piscine, they walked through a blue, misty light through which some of the mosaics became visible. They were there for half an hour, looking at them and discussing what they saw. They saw Peter being saved by Christ after having attempted walking on the water, and others, including Moses bringing forth water from the rock and Jonah and the whale.

Upon their return to Zurich, Jung shared with his students their experience with the mosaics. When a colleague announced a couple of years later that he was going to Ravenna, Jung asked him to take pictures of the mosaics as he and Toni had failed to photograph them. When the man returned to Zurich, he told Jung there were no such mosaics. Jung was stunned. He and Toni had seen them with their own eyes. Later, after much research, they learned that the Empress Galla Placida had made a vow during a terrible winter boat crossing that if she survived, she would have several mosaics created. She did indeed survive, had the mosaics created, and built the Basilica of San Giovanni to house them. Then, in the early Middle Ages, the church and the mosaics were destroyed completely. Jung and Toni had "seen" mosaics that had been gone several hundred years!

Inevitably, Toni began to wish to be an analyst. Jung tried to discourage her, ostensibly because he felt her literary gifts would not find sufficient time for expression. (At one time he compared her poetry to Goethe's.) Possibly he might also have been reluctant because he did not want to "talk shop" with her. A *femme inspiratrice* engaged in the same profession might cease to be inspiring or restful. By 1928, however, he seems to have accepted the inevitable, and at the same time urged her to become president of the Psychological Club. Perhaps he himself was tiring of the complications of their relationship. It's interesting that his interest in alchemy began that same year, and he had found a very willing collaborator in Marie-Louise von Franz, a young student when she first met Jung and who said in an interview with Deirdre Bair that Toni's "big mistake was being not interested in alchemy. It was unfortunate that she refused to follow him there, because otherwise he would not have thrown her over to collaborate with me" (Bair 2003, p. 371).

Whatever the reasons, Toni became the tiger of the Club, supported by Linda Fierz-David, and forced the resignation of a group of members who did not like the direction the Club was taking. This included Erika Schlegel, who had been

Club librarian and even President for a time, and her husband. And most important perhaps, this was the year Jung stopped writing in *The Red Book*. Alchemy was answering many of his questions. Toni kept an eye on everything so that Jung would not be bothered by anyone or anything that did not interest him ... or felt threatening to her. Several members of the Club commented on her intuitive awareness, amounting to psychism, of the atmosphere around Jung.

Her confidence grew, although she never felt entirely happy in groups. Dr. Joseph Henderson commented that of all the people around Jung, Toni, Emma, and Linda Fierz-David kept their shapes best (Henderson 1977). Toni was very much herself, then, and would not be bullied by him. In fact, she developed a knack of putting him in his place when he became inflated by his own self-importance. It was a knack shared by Emma and Linda Fierz-David.

As indicated before, Toni was not at home with women. Aside from Linda Fierz-David, she had no women friends. Every woman with whom I spoke all those years ago described her as intense, intelligent, and beautiful, but none of them spoke warmly of her. Jane Wheelwright said, "If you were a woman she had to lord it over you. If you were a man, it was peaches and cream. I didn't get along with her. I put up with her. But I did work with her" (Wheelwright, Jane 1977). Dr. Joseph Wheelwright, her husband, said simply, "Toni was the best analyst I ever had; better than Jung in my estimation" (Wheelwright, Joseph 1977).

Mary Bancroft, who lived in Zurich with her Swiss husband during the First World War and became a spy for the early CIA, wrote:

> I considered Toni Wolff highly intelligent with a cultured background that impressed me deeply. But I found her personality so unpleasant that I knew I'd pay strict attention to the matter at hand [analysis], so as to finish it as soon as possible. One day she told me that working with me was like wrestling with a boa constrictor.
>
> *(Bancroft 1975)*

Bancroft laughed and Toni was infuriated.

Possibly Toni felt that any woman who turned up in Zurich to work with Jung was a potential rival for his affections. As one source has said, "but on one point their recollections reliably converged: Jung's effect on women was overwhelming" (Donn 1988, p. 171). Certainly most of the women, as well as his female clients, were in love with him, at least a little. The Dionysian side again. The transference was no doubt felt by him as a burden, but could still have been painful for Toni in her special position. And Jung did enjoy the attentions of women. It was said that in his later years he could always be found with the youngest and prettiest women in any gathering, and most often they were Americans.

One woman who was analyzed by Toni, R. A. Lane, had a different picture of her. "She sat at a long, flat-topped desk and you sat, not across from her but at her side. She used to sit there like a little queen and smoked ... with a long black cigarette holder. She had a deep voice.... She was like a mother to me." The same woman goes on to recount how, when she was going home to America, her husband met Toni on the street and told her his wife was "frightened to death, in a terrible panic" over having to travel by plane. And Toni replied very quietly, "Tell her that I don't think the plane will fall down" (Lane 1977).

After Jung built Bollingen Tower, he and Toni would often spend quiet weekends there. At first she did not appreciate the fact there was neither running water nor electricity, but soon she enjoyed it as much as he did and looked forward to their times there. Emma never spent much time at Bollingen.

In describing Toni's personality and appearance, it is easy to forget one fact: her real contribution to the body of Jungian knowledge. Until several years ago her work suffered from lack of translation, and so had not had an audience outside of analytical psychology trainees and teachers. Most of the material she wrote was to be found only in the files of the libraries of the various C. G. Jung Institutes around the world. In my interview with him in 1978, Dr. C. A. Meier spoke of the books being published in Switzerland in German, but now some are available in English, and a few are available online.

One of her earliest known pieces is titled *The Structures of the Feminine Archetype*, which though using the Jungian concept of psychological types as a base, has a few interesting thoughts of her own. It is a valuable work, showing a perceptive intuition about the roles women assume in relation to men. "Here she helpfully proposes that Eros is by no means the leading mode of consciousness functioning in all women" (Rowland 2002, p. 56). This contradicts Jung, who assigned Eros as a female mode with the vision of Salome in *The Red Book*. As Claire Douglas has pointed out, "In Wolff's model, woman's psychology is explored primarily in reference to the way in which she relates to men … these four types also represent a man's anima, one type predominating" (Douglas 2000, p. 205).

This was totally in line with Jung's personality types, not venturing out of the vision of women at the time. A feminist epistemologist, Susan Wyatt, has recently used Wolff's *Structures* in an interesting piece on Medial Women (Wyatt 2017, pp. 25–37).

As the years went on, Toni's relationship to Jung and to Emma stabilized and contemporary memoirs frequently state: "Jung, Toni and Emma did such and such …" or "Jung, Emma and Toni went to such and such …." Part of the reason they were able to make it work as well as it did was due to the heroic efforts of both the women. At one point they both went into analysis with Dr. C. A. Meier, who in my interview with him said only that they both experienced great pain. Perhaps it was the realization on both their parts that neither wished to lose Jung, which helped them adjust to and endure such a painful situation. The triangle continued, though in greatly attenuated form, until Toni's sudden death in 1953.

Jung was shocked by its suddenness. Shortly afterward, on Easter eve, he had a dream about her. She appeared, young and beautiful. Taller than in real life, wearing a dress colored with the hues of a bird of paradise with kingfisher blue emphasized. In Jung's first fantasy of Philemon, who evolved from Elijah, he appeared with the wings of a kingfisher (Lane 1977). Jung had in this dream clothed Toni with the colors of the wise old man of whom she was the natural consort. She had merged with him, as it were. Perhaps he was unconsciously aware that in ancient China the kingfisher was the symbol of fidelity and mated happiness (Harding 2001).

He carved a small stone with an enigmatic message for her in the shadow of the trees at Kusnacht: "Toni Wolff. Lotus. Nun. Mysterious." An epitaph for an anima, indeed.

It is somehow apt that Toni's death was attributed to hitherto undisclosed problems of the heart.

References

Bair, Deirdre (2003) *Jung: A Biography*. Boston: Little, Brown.
Bancroft, Mary (1975) "Jung and His Circle." *Psychological Perspectives: A Quarterly Journal of Jungian Thought* 6(2): 114–127.
Donn, L. (1988) *Freud and Jung: Years of Friendship, Years of Loss*. New York: Scribner's Sons.
Douglas, Claire (2000) *The Woman in the Mirror: Analytical Psychology and the Feminine*. Lincoln, Nebraska: iUniverse. First published Boston: Sigo Press, 1990.
Hannah, Barbara (1976) *Jung: His Life and Work*. New York: Putnam.
Harding, M. Esther (2001) *Woman's Mysteries*. Boston: Shambhala Publications.
Henderson, Joseph (November 1977) Author's interview.
Lachman, Gary (2010) *Jung the Mystic*. New York: Tarcher.
Lane, R. (1977) *A Well of Living Water: Recollections of Toni Wolff, a Festschrift*. Privately printed for Hilde Kirsch's seventy-fifth birthday.
McGuire, William, ed. (1974) *The Freud–Jung Letters*. Princeton, New Jersey: Princeton University Press.
Rowland, Susan (2002) *Jung: A Feminist Revision*. Oxford: Polity Press.
Van der Post, Sir Laurens (1977) *Jung and the Story of Our Time*. New York: Vintage Books.
Wheelwright, Jane (November 1977) Author's interview.
Wheelwright, Joseph (November 1977) Author's interview.
Wyatt, Susan (2017) "Medial Women: Views of a Feminist Epistemologist." In *Feminist Views from Somewhere: Post-Jungian Themes in Feminist Theory*, Leslie Gardner and Frances Gray, eds. Abingdon: Routledge, pp. 25–37.

6

ZURICH PSYCHOLOGICAL CLUB
Edith Rockefeller McCormick

Edith couldn't have arrived at a better time for Jung. She came to Zurich in 1913 after almost a month of daily analysis with Jung in New York, and the same on her voyage to Europe. She came very much in the style one might have expected in that era of the daughter of one of the world's richest men, and the wife of another. Together with her husband, children, a tutor, and a governess, she took possession of a suite of rooms at the very elegant Zurich hotel, the Baur au Lac, where she remained during her almost ten-year stay, living there, and later, as an analyst, seeing clients there.

By all accounts, Edith McCormick had a troubled past, beset by psychological problems, some situational due to the loss of two of her five children in infancy, and herself suffering a debilitating illness. A major emotional symptom was a lifelong battle with agoraphobia. She stayed in her suite at the hotel, very seldom attempting to venture out, and often failing when she did make an attempt. Occasionally, at her husband's suggestion, she would take a hesitant walk with him within the hotel grounds. In addition to her own analysis, her husband Harold became an analysand of Jung's, with a great enthusiasm for the process. He wrote glowingly of it in letters home to his family. He also often accompanied Jung on short walks, and even long walks, averaging 10 to 20 miles a day in the Engadine.

In 1916, Edith leased a very grand building, located in one of the most expensive areas of Zurich. This was to be the Zurich Psychological Club, a central meeting place for Jung's circle and the venue of his lectures on his psychology and research. It was quite grand, modeled on American social clubs, and too pricey for some of its members, who could not afford the accommodations or the dining room. Two years later the Club was moved to the simpler building at Gemeindestrasse 27, which later was to also serve the C. G. Jung Institute for Analytical Psychology until its move to Kusnacht.

With great fanfare, on February 26, 1916, with forty people in attendance including Jung, Emma, and Toni Wolff, the Club opened its doors. The importance of the Club to the furthering of Jung's psychology cannot be overemphasized. As many of Jung's patients at this time were foreigners, coming to live and work with him was not easy in the insular, stranger-wary Swiss society. The Club therefore provided a central meeting place that served to educate his patients in what was to become analytical psychology, and a place to socialize with others in the same position. Not only were they plunging into uncharted regions of the human psyche, they were thrown into a culture that, while not overtly hostile, was distinctly cool toward them. For some time Jung had been concerned about this, and Mrs. McCormick's grand gift seemed like a good solution.

Jung's relationship with Edith McCormick continued for several years and he benefited greatly from her financially. The fact she was seeking treatment with him and finding it beneficial must have attracted other wealthy Americans, too. She was in Zurich with her husband from 1913 to 1923, being analyzed, then herself working as an analyst and studying philosophy. She was also very much a "grande dame" and the author James Joyce did an amusing if malicious sketch of her, perhaps in retaliation for her withdrawal of support, as Mrs. Mervin Talboys in the Circe episode in *Ulysses*. In this, she is portrayed as an exaggerated sort of sadistic society queen sporting a riding-crop. This is possibly one of the few remnants of memory of her left to posterity. Earlier, when she was his benefactress, he had tried to get her to appear in his play *Exiles*, in which he thought her fashionable clothes, jewels, and furs would make her just right for a role he had in mind. She declined to appear, and very possibly not just because of her agoraphobia.

Once the Psychological Club was able to get past Mrs. McCormick's grandiose ideas (which may have stemmed from her membership in very posh American social clubs), it did provide another source of support for Jung's English-speaking followers. Coming so soon after his break with Freud, and his descent into the unconscious, which frightened him and led to *The Red Book* and his relationship with Toni Wolff, the Club must have provided support for Jung himself. It may have been comforting for him to have his own circle of literate, interested people, eager to grasp his ideas as they poured forth from him. The Club also became the place where the various followers of Jung, both analysands and analysts, could come together and find kindred souls in a world when the search for self-knowledge was not widespread. Today, with all the various institutes, forums, centers, and ashrams that proliferated during the late 1960s and into the 1990s, many of which still exist, it is hard to imagine how "ivory tower" this all must have seemed to the world at large. It is no coincidence that the early circle was made up mainly of the well-educated, wealthy upper classes and art world. It is also no coincidence that the circle began so soon after the break with Freud, when Jung was isolated from so many of the colleagues who had broken with him in defense of Freud. From the beginning, Jung used the Club as a place to discuss the material with which he was currently working. In this way, it provided a sounding-board and place where he could introduce new ideas.

Inevitably, there were rituals. For one thing, there were the chairs. From the beginning, three were labeled: "Frau Jung," "Fraulein Wolff," and "Professor Jung." They were not only labeled but upholstered and more comfortable than the wooden ones for the others. If any of the above were not present, it was a rule that their chairs remain empty. One woman, present at early meetings, claimed that a numinous feeling hovered around the chairs. There was also, inevitably, some annoyance at this.

There was also an ice-breaking ritual, which took the form of a game known as "Alleluia." This game simply involved tossing a knotted handkerchief to someone, who caught it and tossed it to someone else. Since the ladies in the Club as a rule dressed very elegantly, and the gentlemen always in dress suits, collars, and ties, it is amusing to think of them playing such a game. Little wonder it took them out of persona and lessened formalities.

If there was a feeling of cult at the Club, as some critics of Jung have alleged, there was also sometimes the sense of it being a battleground. Jung's circle prided themselves on the acceptance of their own shadows and shortcomings, a first step in individuation. The result of this at the Club was that when they were angry they let it be known, and when they were jealous, that was obvious, too. This must have been refreshing in such a conventional society, but it made for some "hot times" at the Club. It was the jealousy that most often came to the surface, though surely any toward Toni was carefully masked given Jung's well-known and observed temper. Maybe the possibility of jealousy displayed was one of the sources of Toni's legendary aloofness, as Jung's publicly acknowledged "other woman."

Early on, there was a conflict of such proportions as to drive Jung himself away for a time. This involved the women, a couple of men within the Club, and Jung himself. Reports vary as to whether Jung and Emma and Toni all walked out, or just Jung. It was after this that Harold McCormick wrote a report for the Club based on his own observations. The last paragraph states:

> I believe that unconsciously there is too much of an atmosphere of rank observed in the club, the mental rank, and the rank between "analytiker" and "analysand." The mantle of "caste" should be laid aside at the threshold of the club and Natural Simple Human Relation assumed in its real aspect.
> *(McCormick n.d.)*

This seemed to help. What might have helped too was the emergence of a very different sort of society, making itself felt in Zurich in that very year, 1916, and which had some definite connections within the club.

Reference

McCormick, H. (n.d.) "The Welfare of the Psychology Club." McCormick Estates Papers, MFM Box 8, File 7, State Historical Society of Wisconsin, Madison.

7
ART ATTACK
Dancing with the Dadaists

In retrospect, it seems Fate stepped into the confines of the Psychological Club upon its 1916 opening. One of the aides to Fate must be seen to be in the person of Erika Schlegel. She and her husband were friends of Toni Wolff, and in 1913 began analysis with Jung. Erika was made librarian of the Psychological Club and later, both she and her husband took turns as president. That Erika was close to Jung and considered among his circle of trusted friends is borne out by the fact that she was one of the very few with whom he shared *The Red Book*.

And it was around that time that Erika's sister, newly returned from textile art studies in Germany, came to stay with them. Sophie Taeuber was one of the leading figures of the Zurich Dada art movement as a dancer and as an artist, and one of their only Swiss-born members. Dada actually mocked the materialistic and nationalistic attitudes that most felt had led to the First World War. And it is particularly interesting that its birth was in Zurich, where both those values were highly valued. It was a deconstructionist art, a deliberate attempt to break down old values and attitudes.

Sophie performed at the celebration of the opening of the Gallery Dada on March 27, 1917, where, as Dada artist Hugo Ball later noted, several members of the Psychological Club were in attendance. Obviously she caught the eye of the membership as Erika's sister, as well as by her dancing in performance. Shortly after this, Sophie and her soon-to-be husband, artist Hans (later "Jean") Arp, were asked to teach a dance class at the Psychological Club. Hugo Ball writes of her performance:

> She is bathed in the brightness of the sun and the miracle that replaces tradition. She is full of inventiveness, whimsy and caprice. She danced to the "Song of the Flying Fish and the Sea Horses," an onomatopoeic lament ... the figures of her dance are at the same time mysterious, grotesque, and ecstatic.
>
> (Ball 1996, p. xxxi)

Heady stuff for the staid and formal Psychological Club members.

The following is an excerpt, quoted verbatim, from a letter from Mme. Jean Arp to American professor and artist Robert Kostka in reply to a query he made in 1975 as to Arp's connection to Jung:[1]

> Clamart, November 25, 1975
>
> Thank you for your letter of November 8.
>
> Regarding the relationship of ARP–JUNG I can only write you the following: Arp always told me that his first wife's (SOPHIE TAUBER-ARP's) sister and brother-in-law (who was a Jungian analyst) founded a psychiatric club with Jung. This club organized once per week a dance in order to liberate the imprisoned libido of its members. Since both Arp and his wife were excellent dancers it was their most unrewarding task to teach the tense professors and the equally tense wives to dance.
>
> Arp also mentioned that Jung had no affinity whatsoever to modern art. As far as I know in one of the books by Jung there are two articles about Art. One of these is about Picasso and shows complete incomprehension for cubism.
>
> Yours very sincerely,
> [signed] Marguerite Arp.
>
> (Arp 1975)

Sophie also received the commission to design and make the puppets and stage sets for a production of the play *King Stag*, by Carlo Gozzi. It was a combination of Dada and psychoanalysis and concerned the battle between Freud and Jung over the nature of the libido. This was staged in Zurich in 1918 and there is no known record of what Jung thought of it, or whether indeed he saw it. But it was sure to have been seen by members of the Psychological Club.

Her sister, Erika, also occasionally took part in Sophie's art projects, the outstanding one being as one of the two dancers, herself and Sophie, adorned in marvelous costumes Sophie had constructed and painted, of human-sized Hopi Kachinas. This took place in 1922, only three years before Jung's trip to America, in which he expressed a desire to see and meet Pueblo Indian people. His description of this meeting, with Ochiway Biano, a Hopi elder, is described at length by Jung in *Memories, Dreams, Reflections* as very important to him. Although the American Indian was greatly admired in popular culture in Europe at the time, especially in Germany, where there were large societies of ordinary German citizens taking Indian names and wearing costumes, it was largely the warriors of the Plains Indians who were the object of admiration. It is interesting to wonder whether the Hopi costumes and dances of Sophie and Erika had a bearing on Jung's choice of visiting the Southwest Pueblo people instead …

Sophie's world fame came late. In the last twenty years art critics and feminist writers have finally seen her as a distinct artist and important member of the Dada movement in her own right, quite apart from her husband Jean Arp, though he promoted her constantly throughout their life together. Her paintings, her costumes, and her puppets have all been on display in museums around the world. As for her dancing:

> [D]ance ... could neither readily nor effectively be transposed into words ... a second possible factor in the neglect of dance is its status as a predominantly female occupation, one in which women have held the expertise. An undercurrent of this is the association of the corporeal with woman and the intellectual with man.
>
> *(Hemus 2009)*

Despite that, Sophie Arp's face is now displayed prominently on the Swiss fifty-franc note, the only woman so honored in Switzerland, where she died in her sleep of accidental gas poisoning at the young age of fifty-four in 1943.

The "romance" between the Dadaists and Jung came to an end around 1919 when he wrote a short piece in a local paper condemning them. A little earlier he had said to Freud, when Freud asked about the Dada movement, "It is too foolish to be able to be insane in some or other decent way" (Van den Berk 2012, p. 103, n. 311).

To the then vulnerable mental state of Jung, who in that period from 1912 to 1920 was undergoing, and writing up in first the Black Books, then the Red, his visionary experiences, not knowing whether the material in them suggested a breakdown or a breakthrough, the impact of the Dadaists must have been profound. Like Jung, the artists within that movement were fascinated by the "'primitive' – a loosely used umbrella term that embraced everything from non-Western art to ancient ritual ... and unconscious states" (National Gallery of Art 2006). The very air in Zurich from 1913 to 1920 was electric with ideas, with the terrible war that surrounded them without physically touching them in their neutrality, and with the breakdown of the old mores. This must have had an even greater impact on Jung because of his personal and professional struggles, including the loss of so many colleagues in the break with Freud. This was the time of his discovery of the mandala, too.

In January of 1916, Jung

> drew a mandala in the Black Books. This was the first sketch of the "Systema Munditorius." He then proceeded to paint this. On the back he wrote in English, "This is the first mandala I constructed in the year 1916, wholly unconscious of what it meant."
>
> *(Jung 2009, p. 42)*

According to one source, Jung must have shortly learned of its healing capacities, as "By 1916, Jung was already telling patients to paint them or even dance them as a way of harmonizing unconscious oppositions.... Arp, encouraged by his wife [Sophie Taeuber], began to experiment with mandalas in 1917" (Repp 2011).

The visionary experiences that initiated the construction of *The Red Book* were themselves to have a lasting impact on the formation of what has come to be called analytical psychology. While some of the first visions were spontaneous, like the blood-soaked vision that presaged the First World War, others were specifically induced by a method used by Jung experimentally, which came to be called by him, eventually in 1935, active imagination. Marie-Louise von Franz considered it the "most powerful tool in Jungian psychology." And Barbara Hannah, in her book on it, *Encounters with the Soul*, has dire warnings of its practice without proper guidance. "Jung did not develop active imagination in a vacuum.... Jung's innovation was nonetheless substantial.... Jung sought the manifestations of symbols and idea that had never before been conscious" (Merkur 1993, p. 53).

They were certainly not developed in a vacuum, as there were indications that some of the artists in the Dada movement used such a tool. And just before the turn of the century, a magical society called the Hermetic Order of the Golden Dawn was instituted in Great Britain and later in Paris. One of the devices used in the training and initiation of new members called "path-working" was for each to attain a sort of twilight state of consciousness, similar to the hypnagogic state, and begin to visualize certain prescribed symbols. There was also a training exercise in which, in that same state, one would simply see which images emerged. Very similar to Jung's initial descent into the unconscious in which he simply let go and dropped down into it. There are also indications that some of what the Golden Dawn taught was based on Gnostic beliefs, as its original founders were also Rosicrucian, which blends Hermeticism with Jewish mysticism and Christian Gnosticism. And all three founders were Freemasons: William Robert Woodman, William Wynn Westcott, and Samuel Liddell MacGregor Mathers. An interesting development, for the times, is that men and women were allowed in the Order as equals.

Jung had been interested in Gnosticism for quite a while and continued to read deeply in what books were available at the time, mostly by Christian clergy critics. "Jung's interest in Gnosticism had begun at least as early as 1902, when his doctoral dissertation, 'On the Psychology of So-Called Occult Phenomena,' described the views of a séance medium as Gnostic" (Merkur 1993, p. 49). Again, it was in the air along with so much else that was surrounding Jung at the time.

And Gnosticism it was that impregnates Jung's *Septem Sermones ad Mortuos*, which he published privately and shared with only a few trusted friends. At the time, in 1916, an associate and friend of Jung's, the analyst Josef Lang, had as a patient Hermann Hesse, a young writer who was in personal crisis. Lang gave Hesse a copy of it, which Jung had sent him knowing certain concepts in it would resonate with his young analysand. It did, so much so that some of these, particularly the god Abraxas, found their way into Hesse's novel, *Demian*. One of the paragraphs in this work shows clear influence of Jung's thought:

> We always define the limits of our personality too narrowly ... but we consist of everything the world consists of ... just as our body contains the genealogical table of evolution ... we bear everything in our soul that was once alive in the soul of man.
>
> *(Shamdasani 2012, pp. 140–141)*

The novel had an impact on Jung, who after reading it sent a letter to Hesse. "Your book hit me like the beam of a lighthouse on a stormy night" (Shamdasani 2012, pp. 140–141).

According to the editor of *The Red Book*, Sonu Shamdasani, Jung recognized that Hesse and he shared some ideas which Jung was working on in his Red Book, and proceeded to contact Hesse further, tantalizing him with the idea that he (Jung) could share even deeper information with him. A few years later, Hesse had a daily session in Zurich during one summer with Jung. And in an essay written shortly afterward, "Artists and Psychologists," he wrote, "The work of Jung is not only an important step forward in the history of a developing science, it is of the greatest value in human practical terms" (Hesse 1918).

It was Jung's theories of the unconscious and particularly the role it played in art that brought him to the attention of Surrealism into which much of Dada had evolved in Paris, after many of the artists moved there after the end of the First World War.

Meret Oppenheim, the much-acclaimed Muse of the Surrealist movement, came from a Swiss family which had close connection with the Jung family. At only fourteen years old, she began to keep records of what she considered significant dreams. She was to say, many years later:

> I've read in Jung how when the chief of a certain tribe had a dream that seemed significant to him, he summoned all his men together and told them about this dream. Because it seemed significant as a whole…. When artists and poets depict what seems significant to them, perhaps it is significant to mankind as well.
>
> *(Eipeldauer, Brügger, and Sievernich 2013, pp. 270–271)*

And later critics of Oppenheim's work have written, "her study of Jung's archetypes and symbols certainly had an impact on the iconography of her work. Many of her motifs and figures – among them the snake, the spiral, the eye, and the mandala – are borrowings from Jung" (Eipeldauer, Brügger, and Sievernich 2013).

Either on his own or through his relationship to Oppenheim, artist Max Ernst came to admire Jung's work, too. He even wrote an alchemical novel, *Une Semaine de Bonté*, which "follows the alchemical process step by step through a 'week' of bizarre images. One of the seven alchemical elements is assigned to each 'day'" (Repp 2011). This was published in 1934, just eight years after Jung had stopped writing in *The Red Book*, following his "discovery" of alchemy through Richard Wilhelm's *Secret of the Golden Flower*. Then Ernst wrote a theoretical essay just a year after the publication of his novel "in which he makes clear references to Jung's psychology of the collective unconscious" (Repp 2011). And it seems that he and Oppenheim even vacationed with Jung during a visit to Switzerland in 1934.

All these references to art and literature and Jung are to point out that especially Jung, vulnerable as he was in the opening two decades of the twentieth century, was certainly influenced by the ideas in the zeitgeist of those times, and in turn was of some influence on them in return. And this certainly influenced the development of his psychology, which he said himself was rooted in the writings and paintings of *The Red Book*. That he strongly denied that the paintings and drawings in *The Red Book* were "art" can be blamed on the woman's voice he heard in his head while contemplating his work that proclaimed "This is art." This seemed to him to be a very dangerous and misleading anima reading of what he was doing and he fought against it into his old age, when he seemed to finally concede that some of his stone sculptures in the tower in Bollingen might well be art. It seems he was as afraid of being seen as an artist as being seen as a mystic. Yet I believe he was both, and a shaman as well.

Note

1 Permission to reproduce the letter here has been granted to the author, Maggy Anthony, and the publisher, Routledge, by the Robert Kostka Estate. Requests/queries may be directed to the Robert Kostka Estate, c/o Andrea Turman, acturman@unr.edu.

References

Arp, Mme. Jean (November 1975) MS Letter to Robert Kostka (American artist, 1928–2005).
Ball, Hugo (1996) *Flight Out of Time*. New York: Viking Press.
Eipeldauer, Simon, Brügger, Ingried, and Sievernich, Gereon, eds. (2013) *Meret Oppenheim Retrospective*. Vienna: Hatje Cantz.
Hemus, Ruth (2009) *Dada's Women*. New Haven and London: Yale University Press.
Hesse, Hermann (1918) "Künstler und Psychoanalyse," quoted in Kevin Repp, *Psyche and Muse: Creative Entanglements with the Science of the Soul* Exhibit, January 28–June 13, 2011, at Beinecke Library, Yale University.
Jung, C. G. (2009) *The Red Book: Reader's Edition*, ed. Sonu Shamdasani. New York: W. W. Norton.
Merkur, Dan (1993) *Gnosis: An Esoteric Tradition of Mystical Visions and Unions*. Albany, New York: State University of New York Press.
National Gallery of Art (2006) "Dada. Cities: Zurich." Washington D.C.: National Gallery of Art. www.nga.gov/exhibitions/2006/dada/cities/zurich.shtm.
Repp, Kevin (2011) *Psyche and Muse: Creative Entanglements with the Science of the Soul* Exhibit, January 28–June 13, 2011, at Beinecke Library, Yale University.
Shamdasani, Sonu (2012) *C. G. Jung: A Biography in Books*. New York: W. W. Norton.
Van den Berk, Tjeu (2012) *Jung and Art: The Autonomy of the Creative Drive*. Abingdon: Routledge.

8

SIEGLINDE

Linda Fierz-David[1]

"[N]o matter how it is brought to us – as a bolt of lightning or as the unexpected, dark beating of wings of a Sophia – we must accept it" (Fierz-David 1988, p. 97). These words written by Linda Fierz-David about the seventh scene in the Villa of Mysteries in Pompeii could well be a description of how she came to be one of Jung's closest collaborators. After staying for four years in a tuberculosis sanitarium in Switzerland around 1923, she had written C. G. Jung to tell him of her dilemma at being away from her husband and four children with no end in sight.

In 1918, after the First World War ended, a flu epidemic spread over Europe, killing thousands of people. Linda became ill with it and almost died. When she finally recovered, it was discovered she had contracted tuberculosis. She had to leave her family of four young sons and her husband to go to a sanitarium in the Swiss Alps. It was a terrible wrench for her and for her family. She had been a devoted mother who every night sang traditional Swiss songs while she accompanied herself on the piano, and told her boys fairy-tales which she herself wrote and illustrated, putting them into little books.

The sanitarium where she was treated was filled with people of many nationalities, many of whom were still being treated for lungs damaged by poison gas used in the war. It sounds very much like the clinic in Thomas Mann's novel, *The Magic Mountain*, where the patients, thrown together by their disease and, very often with only that in common, formed a society all their own. They spoke of all that was happening in the world which was shut off to them, and it was here, ironically, that Linda came to learn of a man in her own home city of Zurich who was a marvelous healer of souls: C. G. Jung. She wrote to him, then went to consult with him, telling him of her life and the fact that she could not seem to find a way out of her illness after four years in the sanitarium. Jung told her to remove herself from the sanitarium, enter a hotel, and heal herself. Years later, in the Houston interview tapes of 1957, shown on television and then released as commercial film, Jung made a statement to the effect that half the number of tubercular cases are psychological, and result from the fact that people under the influence of a complex breathe less deeply. He said, "Some people have very shallow breathing, don't ventilate the apices of their lungs anymore and get tuberculosis" (McGuire and Hull 1987, p. 87). He felt that Linda Fierz-David should resume her academic studies and begin to read books. She followed his advice and within one year was cured of her disease and able to return to her family.

Once home, she found herself in a very complicated situation. Her husband had an Italian cousin who was very witty and very handsome, and cultivated. He gradually became something like a second husband to her, according to her son Heinrich. This was a tortuous situation for her as she remained in love with her husband, who was even more handsome, witty, and charming. The three of them became locked in a complicated relationship and the conflict within her became so strong that once again she went to consult Jung. The most immediate result was that the figure of Jung himself overshadowed that of the cousin, and he came to be the inspirer and "god-like animus" for her. The cousin faded into the background. He did not leave her life altogether, but he was no longer the "second husband."

In fact, Jung entered the life of the entire Fierz-David family. One of Linda's sons, Heinrich, eventually became a Jungian analyst, and his twin brother became an assistant to Wolfgang Pauli, the physicist and close friend of Marie-Louise von Franz and collaborator and friend of Jung. Jung and his wife dined *en famille* with the Fierz-Davids several times, and at a party in their home an event took place which reflects one of Jung's most attractive qualities: his spontaneity.

Hans Fierz-David, Linda's husband, told Jung, "You have just complained that you are so tired by your patients that you have had enough of your practice for the time being. Very well. Tomorrow morning I leave for Egypt and Palestine and I am going first class, which means there is one unused bed on the train and ship. Please join me instead of complaining about your practice." Jung replied he could do no such thing. It was impossible. The next morning, Jung was at the train with suitcases packed. They left together for the Middle East. In Alexandria, they were accosted by a palmist as they left the ship. He read the hand of Professor Fierz-David, then he took Jung's hand. "Oh, you are one of the few really great men that I have met. I cannot say more."

This trip was to have important results for Jung. After their return from the voyage, during which they amply sampled the ship's wine cellar, Fierz-David saw to it that Jung became a professor at the Swiss Federal Polytechnic Institute in Zurich. Here, Jung resumed his academic career.

In the meantime, Linda devoted herself to psychology, and with Jung's encouragement became a Jungian analyst. She also contributed some very fine studies to the body of Jungian knowledge. Her first studies had been in modern literature, and she gave several lectures on the psychological interpretation of literature. Then Jung asked her to work at deciphering a sort of Renaissance sign or picture language used in one of the most famous books of the Renaissance, *The Dream of Poliphilo*, which is composed entirely of pictures from very fine woodcuts. It is also one of the most elusive and expensive volumes in the antiquarian book trade. Linda interpreted it psychologically as the human quest for soul or anima, and gave several lectures on it at the Zurich Psychological Club. Step by step she turned it into a book first published in 1938, then again in 1950. Jung wrote the Introduction to her work on *The Dream of Poliphilo* and said "she leads the reader through labyrinths of obscure symbolism" (Fierz-David 1987). He also speaks of her being his Ariadne, which of course puts him in the role of Dionysus, another mythological theme running through his own personal psychology – and the reason why he was forgiven some of his excesses of temper and indulgence. The book is currently out of print but available from various book dealers.

However, the next major work she completed was an interpretation of the frescoes at the Villa of Mysteries near Pompeii. Linda, or "Sieglinde" as Jung had now nicknamed her, worked hard and did a very feminine, intuitive interpretation of them. In this work "Her vision is clear. And the angle is clearer, she sees from the position of the analyst who has witnessed transformation" (Hall 1988, p. 19). And perhaps a woman who has undergone it herself?

The Villa of Mysteries is a villa just outside Pompeii which houses ten frescoes showing the transit of woman through her life as a young woman, through all the rituals that occur during that time. As an Initiate in the Dionysian mysteries, she goes through this passage, which captures the spiritual meaning behind those events. The frescoes are beautiful, and having been recently restored, very powerful. As M. Esther Harding has written in her Introduction to Fierz-David's book on the frescoes, "Some of the figures give the impression of being portraits of contemporary persons ... while others have a mythological character and yet play a part in the pictured drama" (Harding 1988). And again, "the series is not merely the representation of a myth, but is rather intended to portray the inner or psychological reality of certain mythic happenings.... The experience portrayed on the walls of the Villa represents ... an inner ritual" (Harding 1988). All this Fierz-David speaks of in this book, which is a very woman-oriented view of the ritual journey of Woman. Which is as it should be. She completed this work near the end of her own life, which took place six years before the end of Jung's. She originally presented her findings and material at the Psychological Club where she was a docent until her death. It was originally entitled *Psychological Reflections on the Fresco Series of the Villa of Mysteries, Pompeii: The Initiation Way of a Roman Woman of Imperial Times Interpreted by a Modern Woman from the Standpoint of Jungian Analytical Psychology*. Thankfully this was changed for simplicity upon publication to *Women's Dionysian Initiation: The Villa of Mysteries in Pompeii*.

One wonders whether Jung attended the lecture Fierz-David gave, which would have perhaps provided new insight into his theory of anima and the feminine. As the predominant color in all the frescoes is red, one is reminded that the Mysteries of Woman are blood mysteries all along her life, from birth to death. As a modern feminist writer has written, "the mystery is always of the body. The mystery is always of the body of a woman" (Cixous and Clement 1986) And the revelations of the frescoes underline this. As Nor Hall has written, "the material collected in her manuscript has this God's [Dionysus] flare about it. It is periodically epiphanic. Breakthroughs of emotion, subjectivity and fantasy make her 'scientifically objective' manuscript sparkle" (Hall 1988, p. 17). Fierz-David often appended an apology for these breakthroughs. Considering how much of Jung's own material was gained in just this way, it seems strange that she would feel the need to add any apologies to her treatment of intellectual material. However, it was particularly important to Jung to be thought of as scientific so that his work would be taken seriously. So perhaps Fierz-David was just following in the steps of the Master when she lapsed into subjective stances. It took this particular woman, "whose family had bequeathed her a far-reaching field of interests in politics, poetry ... unconscious Croatian witchcraft, chiromancy and medicine" (Fierz-Monnier 1978), to do such a work perhaps.

Fierz-David had said that a woman needs a man, but she went on to say that if she still sees the source or treasure of herself in him, then she is not ripe for individuation, and this is perhaps why Fierz-David is able to step beyond the bounds of the view of the Jungian concept of the feminine in her work as so many, including her friend Toni Wolff, were unable to do.

In 1953, she contracted stomach cancer. A few months before her death, she called the best dressmaker in Zurich, who had dressed her very elegantly all her life, and had him make her a dress which disguised the distortions to her figure brought on by her illness. She then called a family meeting with her sons. As they arrived, she greeted them from her favorite chair, dressed in the new outfit designed for the occasion. She offered them some sherry and snacks and lit a cigarette for herself to give the appearance of normality. She then proceeded to tell them the contents of her will, including her plans regarding the family properties. They told her they did not at all agree with her plan to give their property, which bordered on Jung's Bollingen estate (which he had originally purchased from the Fierz-Davids), to Marie-Louise von Franz and Barbara Hannah. A compromise was reached whereby the two women received the right, as long as they lived, to visit when none of the sons was in residence. On this property, Linda had built a pavilion, her own Villa of Mysteries. On the walls she had painted "mystic things, a secret language, a secret script," her son remembers, "and she burned a candle in this pavilion."

Toward the end she had to be hospitalized, but for the last two weeks of her life, her son Heinrich Fierz-Monnier came to Zurich and brought her home and remained with her until she died. He felt that Jung's understanding of the special relationship between mother and son enabled him to be closer to her in those last days.

Linda had a little dog to whom she had been much attached as a middle-aged woman. The night this little dog died, she had a dream that a little old man went into the forest and did not return. The night that Linda died, her daughter-in-law had a dream that a little old lady went into the forest and did not return.

She died just six years before the death of the man who she felt had given her back her life more than forty years earlier.

Note

1 Much of the material in this chapter is from a personal interview by the author with Dr.med. Heinrich Fierz-Monnier, Linda Fierz-David's son, in 1978.

References

Cixous, Helene and Clement, Catherine (1986) *The Newly Born Woman*. Minneapolis: University of Minnesota Press.

Fierz-David, Linda (1987) *The Dream of Poliphilo*. Dallas, Texas: Spring Publications.

Fierz-David, Linda (1988) *Women's Dionysian Initiation: The Villa of Mysteries in Pompeii*. Dallas, Texas: Spring Publications.

Fierz-Monnier, Heinrich (1978) Author's interview.

Hall, Nor (1988) *Those Women*. Dallas, Texas: Spring Publications.

Harding, M. Esther (1988) "Introduction." In *Women's Dionysian Initiation: The Villa of Mysteries in Pompeii*, Linda Fierz-David, ed. Dallas, Texas: Spring Publications.

McGuire, William and Hull, R. F. C., eds. (1987) *C. G. Jung Speaking: Interviews and Encounters*. Princeton, New Jersey: Princeton University Press.

9

THE MYSTERIES OF WOMAN

M. Esther Harding

Harding's life had its beginnings in the almost picture-postcard prettiness of the English countryside. The slow-paced, idyllic atmosphere of this part of early twentieth-century Britain seems poor preparation for the almost superhuman struggles she had to endure as that oddity at the turn of the century, the "lady doctor." Yet as she said to a friend at the end of her life, "If you don't understand that I am Shropshire, through and through, you don't understand me at all" (Kennedy 1971). It was possibly that Shropshire strain that stood her in good stead throughout a grueling internship at the Royal Free Hospital in London. It was the only place that accepted women interns at that time. After working inhumanly long hours there, she and her friends would spend any free time listening to the Spanish guitar music that enthralled her at the time. Later, she heard that Stravinsky's *Rite of Spring* was to have its premiere in London, so she saved for months to have a seat at the performance instead of her usual standing room. She said later, "I knew that I was listening to a statement from the New World. High in the gallery that night, I knew the Victorian Age was over" (Van Culin 1971). Very perceptive of her and perhaps not unlinked to her unconscious feeling function, which obviously responded to music. For women like her, few as they were, striving to make a place for themselves in a firmly based patriarchal world, this must have been very good news indeed.

It was perhaps her rigorous medical training and the scarcely believable, in today's world, insults that women in the medical profession had to bear, that made for the stiff discipline she expected of herself and others to the end of her life.

She had been a doctor for six years when she attended Jung's first seminar in England in 1920, held in Sennen Cove, Cornwall. Sennen Cove is a place steeped in mystery, reputed still to be frequented by mermaids, and a sort of "living mist." This is known as the "hooper" for the noise it makes, hovering around the rocks. The locals consider it a protective spirit for the many fisherman of the vicinity. A particularly fitting place for Jung, a "fisher of souls." It was here he found three of his strongest female disciples. The seminar had as its topic the dreams from a book entitled *Peter Blobb's Dreams*. After the seminar, Harding followed Jung to Zurich, as did Dr. Constance Long and Dr. Eleanor Bertine.

After working with Jung in Zurich for three years, Harding came to the United States and joined Dr. Bertine, apparently at the suggestion of Jung. She and Bertine became very close and lived together the rest of their lives. Jung often did a spot of "matchmaking" in this way. He felt that unmarried professional women in careers where they were virtually the only women would need the support of another woman in the same situation. He also sometimes did this with lesbian women for the same reasons.

Once in the United States, Harding, Bertine, and Kristine Mann joined forces and inaugurated the first Analytical Psychology Club in New York in 1936, and were later instrumental in forming the Institute in New York.

Harding ruled the Institute in New York with an iron fist not noticeably in a velvet glove. Anyone who wanted to get involved had to first have a few analytical hours with her. She is seldom spoken of with much affection, except by those who first met her in later years when she had mellowed a bit. Dr. Joseph Henderson, in my interview with him, said she made a distinct effort to bring her feeling function to the fore in those later years. Jung believed that thinking types often lack the conscious ability to feel, and are prone to say things which hurt the feelings of others.

One of the women who worked with her, Margaret Baker, wrote a moving portrait of her in those later years,

> like a wise old bird with that clear high note in her voice, ruffled at times … seemingly lacking in humour, a "thinking type," not a "feeling type" … suddenly there would come a moment of acute observation and the audience would laugh and Dr. Harding would share in the laughter fully like a young girl. The wise old bird had become approachable, the eagle more a gliding and settling gull, but sharp-eyed as ever.
>
> *(Baker 1971)*

Throughout the period of her involvement with analytical psychology, she, Bertine, and Mann would take three-month terms away every year, in rotation, to return to Zurich, to the font, and be analyzed by Jung. Clearly they were among those who needed a renewing lifeline to the great man.

During one of the visits, Harding told Jung of a dream she had once of a priest. Jung told her she had an animus like an archimandrite (the superior of a large monastery of the Orthodox church). "It is as if to say you are a priest of the mysteries. It takes a great humility to balance it. You need to go down to the level of mice" (Harding 1975). This humility was one of the feelings for which she strived.

The work that will ensure her immortality, *Woman's Mysteries*, had its beginnings in the early days with Jung. She attended the English seminars, which he gave regularly in Zurich. In one particular seminar they were studying the dreams of a man, in one of which there was a cauldron in which crescents and crosses were mixed.

Half the seminar members were asked to study the symbolism of the cross, and the other half, that of the crescent. Harding's research was so interesting that Jung encouraged her to enlarge it and write it up for publication. This was the beginning of *Woman's Mysteries*. However, whether due to a remark of Jung's as some have suggested, or to a decision of her publisher, it was many years before it was published.

Dr. Henderson's remarks on an early draft are interesting in this context. "One of the strands of Harding's research had to do with an intoxicating drink known as soma. Jung said, 'First take some of the soma out of it.'" It is as if Esther and the fate of her search obeyed this injunction by withholding publication until her *The Way of All Women* was published. In this work the intoxification of the archetypal imagery has been pushed into the background and the human message alone, maintaining the right balance between theory and practice, shines forth. "Her insights are remarkable for her time (for example, her appreciation of the psychological importance of other women as models, supports, and aids for a woman's personal growth), yet remain unacknowledged by contemporary writers" (Douglas 2000, p. 113).

I was introduced to *Woman's Mysteries* while it was still out of print in the early 1960s by a friend, Brother Antoninus, the Dominican monk and poet. At that time it was almost a cult book taken up by the newly developing women's movement. For me it was nothing short of a revelation of the psychic roots of women. Having only been exposed to Christianity and Judaism, I was stunned to learn that women had once held an honored place in religion and that a female deity in multiple forms had been worshipped. It was no coincidence that it was put into my hands by a poet. Jung was fond of saying that perhaps only poets could really understand him and the same might be said of this work of Harding's.

For me, *Woman's Mysteries* provided an intellectual and historical base for an experience I had had in Brazil only a year or so before being given the book, revealing to me the importance of this work for so many women:

I was initiated spontaneously at a midnight ceremony on a hill in Rio de Janeiro where I lived at the time. I was visiting an Umbanda ceremony with a group of French tourist women, put together by a friend of mine, an Italian Contessa and long-time resident of Rio. The countess had a solid knowledge of the African-based religions prevalent in Brazil, which had been brought by the slaves and blended with Catholicism and a mediumistic strain. She stressed that all the women in the group wear dresses as a sign of respect for the people of the ceremony. Rio is even hot at night in the summer so I wore a white pique knee-length sleeveless dress.

Inside a windowless, dirt-floor shack at the top of a wooded hill, with a huge altar on which were placed many lighted candles, plaster statues of Catholic saints like St. George and Santa Barbara and the Virgin Mary, carved African statues, bottles of cheap sugar-cane liquor and cigars, we were divided into two semi-circles, men on one side, women on the other. This left most of the dirt floor open. Through the doorway, one at a time, would come priestesses, each possessed by a different deity. They entered one at a time and slowly made their way around the half-circle of us who were visitors mixed with regular devotees. They passed close to all of us, in trance and often chanting words in Yoruba, a dialect from Nigeria. At one point, a young priestess, clothed in a long white gown which clung in places to her sweat-drenched body, entered by immediately throwing herself down and "swimming" across the dirt floor to the altar. Then she rose and began to circle the room. She stopped in front of me and I could see the vacant look in her eyes of someone in trance. Something was there in her eyes, but not her. With a lit candle in her hand, taken from the altar, she began to pass it over my arms and between my legs at the knees, muttering in Yoruba. Some drops of hot wax hit my arms but cooled quickly. She came close and looked in my eyes with her vacant, yet not vacant eyes and muttered something, then moved on finally, and out the door. The Contessa whispered to me that Iemanja, the Goddess of the Sea and Moon, had just made me her child. It felt right in my heart, but my intellect kept saying "How is it you feel at home here? You have no African connections, you are not black as most of the devotees are." Coming home to the United States a year later I found my answer in Harding's *Woman's Mysteries*.

> The Moon Goddess belongs to a matriarchal, not a patriarchal system. She is not related to any god as wife or "counterpart." She is her own mistress, virgin, one in herself. The characteristics of these great and powerful goddesses do not mirror those of any male gods, nor do they represent the feminine counterpart of characteristics originally male.
>
> *(Harding, as cited in Douglas 2000, p. 220)*

In her fine book, *The Woman in the Mirror: Analytical Psychology and the Feminine*, Claire Douglas makes some very astute remarks about the book and its relevance even today, to women. "[Harding's] purpose is to present the many sides of the feminine ... especially sides which her culture ignored or devalued" (Douglas 2000, p. 113). And "Harding's emphasis on the power of the archetype and her depiction of it as a strong and important symbol of the feminine stand in implicit contradiction to Jung's and Wolff's view of a related and subservient feminine" (Douglas 2000, p. 113).

> Harding's moon goddesses of the feminine principle have inspired a generation of Jungian feminists because they are virginal in the sense of standing alone, not dependent on any male. Such "Jungian virgins" can be sexual and procreative. Their independence rests in a self-sufficiency generated by contact with the numinous unconscious.
>
> *(Douglas 2000, p. 113)*

Harding, along with Mann and Bertine, spread the Jungian word throughout the eastern United States. She went on to write several more books on Jungian topics; her literary output was perhaps only surpassed by that of von Franz. Along with Bertine and Mann, she was instrumental in setting up the first Bailey Island conference in 1937, at which Jung gave an American seminar.

Although her yearly visits to Jung were the wellspring from which she drew her spiritual and mental energy, the house named Inner Ledges, which she shared with Bertine and Mann on Bailey Island, Maine, was also a source of renewal. There she kept a garden, and among the plants she had a type of ground cover native to her home in Shropshire, which she encouraged to grow in Maine. Like herself, it seemed to thrive in its adopted land.

In the last years of her life she took to wearing a black felt hat, regarded by those who saw her in it with astonishment and horror. In this monstrosity, combined with outsize black glasses to protect her eyes, she set out for what was to be her last journey. One of her friends took her to the airport, feeling that the whole ensemble gave her a "forbidding, Fellini-like look" (Kennedy 1971). The trip was her first to Greece, the home of the women's mysteries of which she had written. She also got to see the stone tower Jung had built himself at Bollingen, which for one reason or another she had never managed to see on her visits to Jung. Her last stop was the family home in Shropshire, which she had not visited in ten years. A few days later, in the airport hotel, she died in her sleep. She was eighty-three years old.

She left a fortune of 1 million dollars to the New York Institute when she died. She may well be judged, by generations of women, to have made the most outstanding contribution to the literature of women's psychology.

References

Baker, Margaret (1971) "Images of Transformations." *Quadrant* 11(Autumn), Esther Harding Memorial Issue.

Douglas, Claire (2000) *The Woman in the Mirror: Analytical Psychology and the Feminine.* Lincoln, Nebraska: iUniverse. First published Boston: Sigo Press, 1990.

Harding, Esther (1975) "Esther Harding's Notebooks." *Quadrant* 8(Spring).

Kennedy, W. (1971) "Esther Harding: To Greece and Home." *Quadrant* 11(Autumn), Esther Harding Memorial Issue.

Van Culin, R. (1971) "Esther Harding and Stravinsky." *Quadrant* 11(Autumn), Esther Harding Memorial Issue.

10
THE AMERICANS
Eleanor Bertine and Kristine Mann[1]

Since Bertine and Mann spent so much of their lives together and shared so much, it seems only fitting that they should share a chapter in this book.

Mann was fourteen years Bertine's senior and both were born in the eastern United States. Mann's parents were Swedenborgians. This was a mystical Christian sect founded in the nineteenth century by Emmanuel Swedenborg. Her father, Charles Holbrook Mann (1839–1918), was "in his day the chief intellectual of the Swedenborgian New Church in America … in his book, *Psychosis* (1900) Mann attempted to formulate a doctrine of the healing of the body through the soul" (Webb 1976, p. 389). A fit background for his daughter, Kristine, who was to become one of Jung's closest followers and leading proponents in the United States.

Kristine Mann graduated from Smith College in 1899 and proceeded to teach science, history, and English at various schools, including Briarly School of New York and Vassar. She then decided on a medical career and graduated from Cornell in 1913.

In the meantime, one of the young women whom she had taught at Vassar, Eleanor Bertine, graduated summa cum laude and Phi Beta Kappa from that college. Bertine announced to her parents that she intended to go to medical school, and they begged her to reconsider; medicine was not considered a fit career for a woman in those times. She thought it over for a year at their request, then went on to Cornell Medical School, where she was one of only three women in the class. Mann was one of the other two.

Mann's chief interest was health education for women, and on graduation from medical school she worked in that area. Meanwhile, Bertine did an internship at Bellevue Hospital in New York and was interested in psychology from the beginning. She was also a consulting physician at the New York Reformatory for Women. She found the conditions there so terrible, she resigned in protest.

After the First World War, Bertine played a key role in putting together a program for an international conference for women physicians for the War Work Council of the YWCA. Women doctors came from more than fifteen countries to hear lectures on such subjects as health and morality in the light of the new psychology. Her views were quite advanced for the time, as remarks such as the following indicate: "I can conceive of circumstances under which a so-called immoral act might be a real step toward the development of an individual." Very heady stuff for a society that was only just beginning to lift the hem of the skirt to a workable length.

Both she and Mann seemed to have been influenced at the time by another woman doctor practicing at Cornell Medical School: Dr. Beatrice Hinkle. Dr. Hinkle had moved east from San Francisco, where she had been the first woman to hold a public health position as City Physician. Upon her arrival in New York, she opened the first psychotherapeutic clinic in America at Cornell Medical School. Shortly after, she went to Europe to investigate the work of C. G. Jung, who was then a new name in psychiatry. She can be seen in the familiar photograph of the Weimar Congress, standing near Emma and Jung.

Hinkle was so impressed by Jung that she undertook the first English translation of his *Psychology of the Unconscious*. And subsequently found a publisher. She thereby launched Jung's American reputation and was instrumental in making him available to many English-speaking people who otherwise would not have had access to his work. As time went on, her translation was found not to be as precise as Jung wished and that of C. F. Baynes, the wife of Peter Godwin Baynes, supplanted it. Both she and her husband had done a great deal of translating of Jung's work. Hinkle also undertook to write a book with a similar typology to Jung's but differing on many critical points. Though she remained an analyst and a friend of the three New York women, including Harding, she was never thought of as a Jungian again.

In 1920, Eleanor Bertine went to England for analysis along with Dr. Constance Long. Long was one of those responsible for bringing Jung to speak at the first seminar in England, at Sennen Cove. It was attended by only twelve people, a number Jung found most congenial. It was there Bertine first met Jung, as well as meeting Dr. Esther Harding. She was so impressed by Jung she followed him back to Zurich, as did Harding. She remained there for a couple of years, studying and undergoing analysis. She wrote to her friend Kristine Mann, who then went to Zurich herself in 1921, there to study with Jung.

It was possibly during this time, and in later visits and analysis with Jung, that Mann painted a series of mandalas that became the focus of his well-known essay, "A Study in the Process of Individuation." It was she, identified only as "Miss X" by Jung, whose paintings and case were presented at the very first Eranos conference in 1933, then published in the *Eranos Jahrbuch* the following year. After much editing and re-working, the essay was again published in Volume 9, Part 1 of Jung's *Collected Works*. This version includes twenty-four of Mann's paintings, of which another forty-eight exist in the Jung Institute Picture Archive in Kusnacht, Switzerland (Darlington 2015).

In 1922, Drs. Hinkle, Mann, and Bertine, who remained lifelong friends, returned to the United States to pioneer Jungian analysis on the east coast. Dr. Constance Long was with them but died an untimely death shortly after arriving. Dr. Harding joined them in 1923. Bertine and Harding took an apartment together and gave small dinner parties, invitations to which were highly prized. Together with Mann, they founded the New York Analytical Psychology Club in 1936, and also planned Jung's Bailey Island Seminar in 1927. One hundred people showed up, which rather overwhelmed Jung, who preferred small gatherings. After it was over, he and Emma arrived in England quite exhausted by all the people and activities.

Bertine wrote two books on Jungian psychology, *Men and Women* and *The Conflict of Modern Woman*. Unlike her roommate Harding's work, Bertine's books stay close to the Jungian concept of the feminine and the anima, and woman's role as seen by the patriarchal culture. Much of her work creatively extends and elaborates Jung's essay "Woman in Europe" (1927).

All three women led long, productive, and creative lives, supporting one another and remaining close to Jung. Dr. Mann died in 1945 at the age of sixty-three. While still an analyst and still active in the club, Dr. Bertine died in 1968, aged eighty-one. Dr. Harding lived the longest, dying in 1971, her eighty-third year, after fulfilling (as we have seen) her lifelong ambition of going to Eleusis in Greece, where the Great Goddess had ruled supreme.

The part played by these women in widening the influence of Jung's psychology cannot be overestimated. Jung valued them and their work and kept in regular contact until his own death in 1961. That they were forbidding and difficult is certainly true, but given their contributions, much can be forgiven.

Note

1 Much of the information in this chapter comes from Darlington 2015.

References

Darlington, Beth (2015) "Kristine Mann: Jung's 'Miss X' and a Pioneer in Psychoanalysis." *Spring: A Journal of Archetype and Culture* 92(Spring): 371–399.

Webb, James (1976) *The Occult Establishment*. La Salle, Illinois: Open Court Publishing Co.

11

ERANOS

Olga Fröbe-Kapteyn

One of the least well known, but perhaps one of the most influential women around Jung, was Olga Fröbe-Kapteyn, who founded Eranos, which became an annual gathering of the best minds in the fields of religion, mythology, anthropology, and psychology. Eranos also became a showcase for the most scholarly people of the time, including one of the most influential, Jung. He is credited with giving her the idea, some say in analysis with her, while others maintain she never was in analysis with him but encountered him at Keyserling's School of Wisdom and asked his advice about an auditorium space she had built on her property but could not find a proper use for. Jung, noticing she was an extravert and deep in studies of various Eastern religions and philosophies, suggested she might use it as a meeting place between East and West. And thus, the idea of Eranos came into being.

Frau Fröbe-Kapteyn was Dutch, born in London, of intellectual parents and lived in Bloomsbury until her twelfth year, when, because of his business interests, her father moved the family to Zurich. After graduation from the University of Zurich, in 1909 she married the orchestra conductor Iwan Fröbe, with whom she had twin daughters. One twin was born severely disabled and spent her life in an institution. Fröbe-Kapteyn visited her regularly until sometime after Hitler took power, when Fröbe-Kapteyn came to see her and found her daughter missing. There were rumors she had been taken with others who were severely challenged as part of Hitler's "cleansing of the race." Fröbe-Kapteyn never saw her again. Five years later, Fröbe-Kapteyn's husband died. Together with her daughter Bettina, she moved to southern Switzerland, into Casa Gabriella in Ascona on the shores of Lake Maggiore, which her father had willed to her.

She immediately plunged into studies of a metaphysical sort, including Theosophy. She was close to Alice Bailey, one of the leading Theosophists, and even sponsored a seminar that Bailey held at the same place where Eranos was to begin a year or so after. Jung was very wary of Theosophy and told Fröbe-Kapteyn so. But her studies were vast and included Eastern philosophies and religions. And her curiosity led her to many places and to knowing many of the leading lights of several mystical sects. It was at the Casa Gabriella that she built the meeting hall, which Jung suggested she use for intellectual gatherings to discuss the very topics in which she was interested.

Thus the very first Eranos conference in 1933 took place, titled "Yoga and Meditation East and West." One of the later participants has written that "Olga Fröbe Kapteyn's demand that academic research be united with personal experience in the sense of mental and spiritual renewal" was one of the guiding lights (Hakl 2013, p. 57). Fröbe-Kapteyn herself wrote:

> Might not ... Eranos be compared to the Gnostic Schools of Mystery teaching to groups like the Essenes ... to the schools of Plato and Pythagoras, to eastern schools of Yoga which were concerned with the sciences of the soul, with man's Quest, and with the extension of consciousness?
> *(Fröbe-Kapteyn 2015, p. 35)*

Jung himself was so impressed with the lineup of scholars who agreed to attend and speak at that first conference that he too accepted her invitation to speak. "You devil! You've invited all my friends and colleagues! Of course I'll come!" he is reported to have said.

Among the conference delegates was Dr. Rudolf Otto, author of *The Idea of the Holy*, who gave the conference its name. Eranos is a Greek word meaning a feast to which everyone brings his own offering. Jung's offering for this first conference was an empirical study of the process of individuation. Toni Wolff made a copy of this speech which can be found in the *Collected Works*. And so the Eranos Tagung began, a yearly conference presented at Frau Fröbe-Kapteyn's Casa Gabriella.

Thus began for Jung a very fruitful annual event at which he was able to meet many people he might not otherwise have encountered, and where he began many of his closest associations with other scholars. It also gave him another place to try out new material on which he was working. This also might have been the reason for the alleged ill feeling toward Frau Fröbe-Kapteyn from many of the Psychological Club around Jung who considered her an outsider, not one of the circle. However, American psychotherapist Ira Progoff has written:

> I had observed that each time Jung spoke at Eranos it seemed to become the occasion for breaking new ground in his thinking. Certainly the thought occurred to me that perhaps the atmosphere of Eranos had something to do with it.
> *(Progoff 1966, p. 307)*

Jung also suggested to Fröbe-Kapteyn that she travel and collect archetypal images. She had great success doing this and the Eranos collection was particularly rich in images of the Great Mother. This archetype was quite important to her personally. In a letter to British occultist and author Dion Fortune, she wrote that she "found she could easily enter into a kind of 'waking trance' in which mythical images would surface, all of them having some connection with the Great Mother" (Hakl 2013, p. 57). In the late 1940s she asked Erich Neumann to write a catalog of these images. Interestingly, Neumann had already had his own encounter with this archetype when he first arrived in what would become Israel. "[He] discovered to his astonishment an archetypal connection with the land. He describes how his anima started to connect to the earth, suddenly 'appearing in dreams all nice and brown, strikingly African, even more impenetrable in me, domineering'" (Liebscher 2015, p. xx). This "catalog" grew and became one of his finest, best-known books, *The Great Mother: An Analysis of the Archetype*. Fröbe-Kapteyn and Neumann had a close intellectual relationship and she was devastated by his early death.

The atmosphere at Eranos was not, as one might expect, that of a scholarly ivory tower. For one thing, all the women around Jung flocked to it, not only to hear him speak, but for a chance to speak to him. Several people at the early conferences complained they were hardly able to get near him because he was always surrounded by female admirers who came to be called the "Jungfrauen." Dr. F. M. Cornford of Oxford University was told by Indologist and art historian Heinrich Zimmer, "Don't go to Ascona: the *fohn* blows all the time and it is full of ladies with transferences." It scared Cornford enough that he turned down his invitation to speak. The *fohn* is a legendary Swiss wind that blows off the Alps and is blamed by the Swiss for everything from nervous tension to sinus headaches.

As far as the "ladies with transferences," one of the women described the scene thus, "when the lecture was over, Jung used to sit on this wall and in a flash we were clustering around him like bees around a honey-pot, much to the annoyance of the other participants" (Jaffé 1989, p. 135). Note the bee imagery, which conjures up the idea of the priestesses of Aphrodite, surrounding Apollo. But if he could be a modern stand-in for the Sun God, he could also summon up echoes of Dionysus.

This god was in evidence at the Night of the Maenads, which gained some notoriety as the only time at which the revels of the conference came close to getting out of hand. From all accounts, the noise was the major disturbance, and rose to such a pitch that the neighbors (not exactly next door to such an estate), complained and called in the local police. Jung himself was running around, making toasts, embracing the women, laughing his famously uproarious laugh, and baptizing a few with libations of wine. A Dionysian revelry to be sure. It lasted all night, and it is said that Frau Fröbe-Kapteyn, herself a teetotaller, made sure that such events never happened again.

If Jung once more had the good fortune to receive from a woman as much or more than he gave, he also found Frau Fröbe-Kapteyn useful in another way. Over the years, as an adjunct to Jungian analysis, he developed a technique known as active imagination. Simply defined, this is a process to which material and images from dreams and fantasies are pictured in the mind's eye, and then allowed to unfold with little or no conscious urging. In this way, his analysands very often got the opportunity to work out unfinished dreams that were still troublesome, to see what unexpressed fantasies are present in the unconscious, and to dialogue with this material. In his essay on this process, Jung gives many warnings concerning the dangers of the technique, and the need for the guiding hand of the analyst. For many, however, the dangers could not even be imagined as they were unable to do it at all. According to the San Francisco analyst Dr. Joseph Henderson, people who were stuck in their inability to relate to the unconscious would be sent to Frau Fröbe-Kapteyn by Jung. She was highly intuitive and almost mediumistic and when people would come to her from him, she wouldn't do a thing. They would just sit in the room with her and spontaneously begin to have active imagination. "It happened to me once in her house. I just suddenly began to have visions!" (Henderson 1977). It was she who said, "The deepest things in human life …can only be expressed in images" (Fröbe-Kapteyn 2015, p. 9). And *Visions*, an impressive collection of 300 images drawn by her using the Jungian technique of active imagination between the years of 1934 and 1938 was recently published. Interestingly, she was never in analysis with Jung, though they had a few early meetings. In 2016, in the New Museum in New York, several of her paintings were on display in a show entitled The Keeper. The individuals whose work was in this exhibit didn't identify themselves as artists or even call what they made art. Fröbe-Kapteyn called her works "meditation drawings" and they date from the 1920s and 1930s (Progoff 2006).

There was clearly more to Frau Fröbe-Kapteyn than was realized, though. Gershom Scholem, philosopher and historian, wrote, "When we, Adolf Portman, Erich Neumann, Henri Corbin, Mircea Eliade, Karl Kerenyi and many others – scholars of religion, psychologists, philosophers, physicists and biologists – were trying to play our part in Eranos, the figure of Olga Fröbe-Kapteyn was crucial – she whom we always referred to among ourselves as The Great Mother" (Hakl 2013, p. 12).

She continued to present the Eranos conferences year after year, editing the Eranos yearbook from 1933 to 1961, until her death in 1962, shortly after Jung's death.

References

Fröbe-Kapteyn, Olga (2015) "The Psychological Background of Eranos." *Eranos: Its Magical Past and Alluring Future*. Special Issue of *Spring: A Journal of Archetype and Culture* 92: 9–11.
Hakl, Hans Thomas (2013) *Eranos: An Alternative Intellectual History of the Twentieth Century*. Montreal: McGill-Queen's University Press.
Henderson, Joseph (November 1977) Author's interview.
Jaffé, Aniela (1989) *From the Life and Work of C. G. Jung*. Einsdeln, Switzerland: Daimon Verlag.
Liebscher, Martin, ed. (2015) *Analytical Psychology in Exile: The Correspondence of C. G. Jung and Erich Neumann*, Philemon Foundation Series. Princeton and Oxford: Princeton University Press.
Progoff, Ira (1966) "The Idea of Eranos." *Journal of Religion and Health* 3(4): 307–314.

12

THE ALCHEMIST'S DAUGHTER

Marie-Louise von Franz

She was perhaps the most introverted of all of the women in Jung's circle, maybe due to the fact that she came to him as early as she did and bonded so thoroughly. In a BBC centenary celebration of Jung, she gave a rare interview and spoke of their first meeting.

> Suddenly out of the bushes, came what seemed like an enormous man with a dirty shirt, dirty trousers, and gold rimmed spectacles and I thought, "What an incredible face he has." He was very friendly. I was terribly shy and he just shook our hands and said, "I haven't finished cooking. You boys go down and look at the lake and my sailing boat down there." And then he called me and said, "Could you cut these cucumbers up?" In great excitement I did, and cut my thumb and the blood ran into the cucumber. And Jung just roared with laughter and gave me a bandage and everything began.
>
> *(BBC 1975)*

In her oral account, von Franz takes on the tone of voice of that eighteen-year-old girl she had been. What she doesn't say is that Jung changed the course of her life profoundly and to his own ends. "Jung knew as soon as he met her that she had a particular kind of intelligence he needed to put to work for him" (Bair 2003, p. 369). And "he followed his usual pattern with women and put her to investigate a special area where he needed research assistance ... classical languages and literature" (Bair 2003, p. 369).

Von Franz then changed her major at university and did what Jung suggested.

> For a few minutes, I thought, "Now am I crazy or is this man crazy? I can't see what he is driving at." Until I realized that for him the soul was real and

> I became tremendously enthusiastic. We stayed until midnight and he poured a lot of wonderful Burgundy down us and so I came home completely happy.
> (BBC 1975)

By her own account, the transference to Jung was very deep and profound.

Sometime later, von Franz was having some difficulties psychologically and asked Jung if she could go into analysis with him, though she could not really afford it. He agreed to take her on without charge in exchange for her translations from Latin and Greek alchemical texts. She readily agreed. This was in the 1930s just as his focus was changing and his interest in alchemy taking over. So, at nineteen she literally became his confidante in a way that Toni Wolff had before her, and she even boasted, "intellectually I replaced Toni Wolff in Jung's life" (Bair 2003, p. 371). Von Franz graduated from the University of Zurich, later earning her doctorate in classical philology, magna cum laude.

She became his collaborator in his alchemical researches to the extent that she translated one of the most valuable works in alchemy, *The Aurora Consurgens*. And her work was so involved with his that "the first German edition of *Mysterium Coniunctionis* was published in a three-volume work with von Franz as co-author ('unter Mitarbeit von Dr. phil. M-L von Franz'). Followers objected strongly" (Douglas 2000, p. 120). It was said later that she was bitterly disappointed when *The Aurora Consurgens* was not included in Jung's *Collected Works* and, of course, this earlier recognition of her work would have been part of the reason. It also shows how closely she identified her work with his.

She was born in 1915, the daughter of an Austrian nobleman who came to Zurich three years later to live and raise his family. She was the youngest of the women around Jung and made the biggest impact on the other Jungians. She is chiefly known now for her multiple writings on the interpretation of fairy-tales, as well as her writings on alchemy and on numerology. She also considered herself an authority on what Jung would or would not have approved of in matters at the C. G. Jung Institute in Zurich and other Jungian domains. This was brought home to me personally during my studies at the Institute in 1972–1973, when a course on group therapy was offered and von Franz walked out and refused to teach that year. Some of her followers, such as Barbara Hannah, also refused. Eventually the Institute relented and withdrew the course. She said her reason for objecting was that Jung had come out against the group process in his lifetime, which he had. What she did not take into consideration was that this was a good twelve or thirteen years after his death and that over and over again Jung had changed his mind as he researched and gathered more evidence on a variety of subjects.

Ultimately it was von Franz whom Jung asked to complete the work his wife had started on the Grail. Emma Jung had begun it because an ancestor had failed in his quest for it, so she said, yet others felt it was her intent to fully understand her husband's work that was the impetus. Von Franz and Emma were never close, but as his wife lay dying, Jung encouraged von Franz to see her because "her attitude toward you has changed." In any case, Emma asked von Franz to take on the work. Von Franz admitted to being concerned to take on someone else's "child." Then she had a dream in which Mrs. Jung gave a bowl of soup to her dog and von Franz interpreted this as meaning Emma was feeding her mother instinct, indicating she could carry Emma's "baby" to birth. The book was published in 1980 as *The Grail Legend* by Emma Jung and Marie-Louise von Franz. It is a fine book.

Ambivalent feelings seemed to flourish around von Franz, as they did about many of the Jungian circle. One Jungian I interviewed spoke of "the strain of being around her because she is so brainy." Of course her first function was thinking, and thinking types, with feeling as their most inferior function, often step on the feelings of others, often quite unconsciously. Also relevant, of course, is the "freeze" she put on the continued growth and development of Jung's ideas.

This is particularly true in her writing on women, the feminine, and the anima. All of her ideas adhere strictly to Jung's view, which, as we have seen, was conditioned by the times in which he was born and his own particular psychological makeup. "The emphasis of her writings is on the via negativa. She tends to dwell on the shadow side of her women patients" (Douglas 2000, p. 121). Further, "This apparent denial of a woman's right to her own good thinking is a crucial problem in the conservative reading of analytical psychology that negatively impinges on female analysands and readers, and undermines a woman's own self-esteem" (Douglas 2000, p. 121). A woman of her intellect and with her relationship to Jung could have perhaps done much to enlighten the Master about a different way of looking at the psychology of woman. But as a reading of her works, particularly the interpretations of fairy-tales, shows often, his views dominated her own. In *The Feminine in Fairytales*, she writes, "Many young girls refrain from studying or developing their minds because they *rightly* feel [italics mine] they would fall into animus possession and that would prevent them from marrying" (Von Franz 1993, p. 83). Even a woman's intellect is not hers and has to be attributed to a complex, it seems. Later in the same work, she writes rather poignantly and personally of the loneliness of such a life and how a woman needs to accept it. "According to my experience, it is very painful, but very important for women to realize and accept their loneliness" (Von Franz 1993, p. 83).

Late in the 1950s a relationship of sorts developed with the world-renowned physicist Wolfgang Pauli, who began a correspondence with her and had several meetings with her. He was a close friend of Jung's, yet there is some doubt as to whether Jung knew of his relationship to von Franz.

When they met in 1947, she did help Pauli with translations of Kepler and Fludd. "Their relationship changed character around 1957 and developed into a more personal and passionate one, at least on Pauli's side" (Gieser 1996, p. 145). Though we have his letters to von Franz, unfortunately hers to him were destroyed by his wife, who came upon them shortly after his death and thought they were from a lover.

Pauli obviously felt a strong affinity with her as he was born in Austria too, and because both of them were thinking types, often misjudged as cold by others.

Pauli had definite views about women not belonging in science, and seems to have had views of women and the anima quite similar to Jung's, though he was Jung's junior by twenty-five years. This would have fit in well with von Franz's thinking. "C. A. Meier judged von Franz harshly, saying she totally misunderstood Pauli, failing to appreciate his efforts to conduct an analytic dialogue with her and that their relationship was tragic" (Gieser 1996, p. 151).

Everyone agrees on one thing about von Franz – her brilliance. But it is a brilliance that can be maddening and obscure at times, one that takes it for granted that the reader has read all the same sources and is as erudite as she. Her biography of Jung was long awaited, but when it appeared it was so laced with alchemical symbols and references from mythology and fairy-tales that many people, Jungians included, became lost in its obscurities and couldn't find the man.

Although she lived with the Jungian lay analyst and writer Barbara Hannah for years at Jung's suggestion, von Franz was very much a loner. She had built a tower for herself near Jung's at Bollingen and spent her most peaceful and pleasant times there. She felt close to Nature, which she felt was woman's natural domain. "Women have a very deep relationship to Nature in its positive form" (Von Franz 1993, p. 86).

Von Franz seems to have been closer to Jung in his last years than anyone other than his family. And she felt responsible for carrying on his work. She once told of a dream of hers in which a stack of Jung's writings on alchemy dropped to the ground and a tremendous wind came up and started blowing them all away. She had to run around collecting them and putting them together all over again. This dream is very symbolic of how she viewed herself and her relationship to Jung. Perhaps it is why she clung so tenaciously to his written word, and feared that any new ideas, such as the group class at the Institute, would "blow all the papers away." In some way, though the winds of change may come and scatter his work, she is the one who tried to hold it all together. Quite a task for a woman who was so ill with Parkinson's disease for twelve years before her death.

In Jung's last days, she was privy to the last visions he had. In the film *A Matter of Heart*, she revealed a vision of some importance.

> Interviewer: Jung had a vision at the end of his life of a catastrophe. It was a world catastrophe.
> Von Franz: I don't want to speak much about it. One of his daughters took notes and after his death gave them to me. And there is a drawing with a line going up and down, and underneath it. It is the last fifty years of humanity, and some remarks about a final catastrophe being ahead. But I have only these notes. Jung never thought that we might do better than just possibly get round the corner with not too big a catastrophe. When I saw him last, he had a vision while I was with him, but there he said, "I see enormous stretches devastated, enormous stretches of earth. But, thank God, it is not the whole planet."
>
> *(Wagner 1986)*

On Death and Dying was her last work. Because of the state of her health while writing it, much was focused on this theme.

> It is only now that I have dreamed it is finished, and I've done my work, that I see the pattern. In old age, one turns away from outer activity more, and one begins to reflect and summarize whatever one has done up until now, and what for, and has it any meaning or is it meaningless ... a certain fear of death which makes one prepare to be concerned with death ... what is life, what is the meaning of life, why have I lived ... was it worthwhile.
> ...
> [P]robably the reason for my illness. I've overworked all my life, my illness is an exhaustion illness.
>
> *(Segaller and Berger 1989)*

In 1986, she gave one of her last lectures, *The Conference of the Birds*, and one analyst was surprised to find it given with such feeling, not displayed in the past by von Franz (Beebe 2009).

I was very frustrated when writing this chapter that I had not been able to interview von Franz myself due to the interference I've mentioned previously by a San Francisco woman analyst who thought it impertinent of me to write about the Jungian women at all. A dream reassured me that von Franz had brought her feeling function into her life near the end.

She died in February 1998 at her home in Kusnacht, aged eighty-three.

References

Bair, Deirdre (2003) *Jung: A Biography*. New York: Little, Brown.
BBC (1975) *Centenary Celebration of Jung's Life*.
Beebe, John (2009) "Once More with Feeling." *Jung Journal* 3(4): 28–39. DOI.org/10.1525/jung.2009.3.4.28.
Douglas, Claire (2000) *The Woman in the Mirror: Analytical Psychology and the Feminine*. Lincoln, Nebraska: iUniverse. First published Boston: Sigo Press, 1990.
Gieser, Suzanne (1996) *The Innermost Kernel: Depth Psychology and Quantum Physics*. Berlin: Springer Books.
Segaller, Stephen and Berger, Merrill (1989) Marie-Louise von Franz interview. In *The Wisdom of the Dream, The World of C. G. Jung*. [Film.] London: RM Associates.
Von Franz, Marie-Louise (1993) *The Feminine in Fairytales*. Boston: Shambhala Publications.
Wagner, Suzanne (1986) *A Matter of Heart*. [Film.] Los Angeles: C. G. Jung Institute.

13

IMPRESARIA

Jolande Jacobi

She was, perhaps, the most controversial of the Jungian women. In part this was due to her being the lone extravert in a sea of introverted women. And it was obvious that Jung had some mixed feelings about her; the relationship always felt a bit chancy. In my interview with the California analyst Dr. Joseph Wheelwright in the 1970s, he told of an incident to which he was a witness. He had been coming to Jung for analysis at eight o'clock every morning. Because of the demands on his time, Jung was seeing patients even earlier. On one occasion, as Dr. Wheelwright started ascending the stairs to Jung's office,

> I heard the above door bang open as if it had been charged by a buffalo and I heard Jung yelling, "raus! raus! raus!" (out! out! out!) and the next thing I heard as I walked up the stairs, electrified by this bellow, was the unmistakable sound of a woman's bottom going "bump bump bump" down the stairs. I arrived at the middle landing at the same time that she [Dr. Jacobi] arrived on her bottom from the top of the stairs. Her skirts were up over her head. She got up (she was not easily shy or embarrassed) and pulled her skirts down to where they were supposed to be ... and she bowed to me and said, "Gruezi, Herr Doktor," and I said, "Gruezi, Frau Doktor," and she walked down the stairs, this time on her feet. [Upstairs when I arrived] Jung was pouring quarts of spit out of his pipe stem, which he did when annoyed. When he wasn't doing this he was running up and down the office. I said, "Is it indiscreet of me to ...?" He said, "No! It is not indiscreet! She came here saying she wants to write a book. But that's not it. She wants to pick my brains and she wants analysis with me!"
>
> *(Wheelwright 1977)*

This incident would have occurred in the 1930s, shortly after Jacobi arrived from Austria, where she had received her degree, at great personal danger to herself.

Several years earlier, she had met Jung at the Kulturbund in Vienna, where she was vice-president. One of her duties was to arrange lectures by famous people in the arts in Europe. In the visitor's book, which she kept from those days, one reads: "Bela Bartok, Paul Valery, Heinrich Zimmer and ... Jung." For Jung, she gave a luncheon in her apartment for him and his admirers. After all the others had left, Jung stayed behind and spoke to her of the *I Ching*. She was impressed that he could write out all sixty-four hexagrams by heart.

Later on that year she had a dream that shook her profoundly, and later she was to write about that dream, ascribing it to an anonymous woman, thirty-eight years old. She writes that the woman knew nothing of psychology at that time and was profoundly shaken by the dream. The dreamer finds herself in a baroque castle with twelve sides, mirrors lining all sides and the ceiling. She finds herself lying fully clothed in the middle of the floor that is, at first, revolving slowly. In the center was a metal knob to which the dreamer clung. The multiple reflections of herself confused her to the point where she felt a loss of identity. Then the floor spun so fast that she experienced vertigo. And in its speed, her clothes were torn away and she feared she would lose her hold on the knob. Nude and frightened, she was flung against one of the mirrored walls, which "shattered and seemed to engulf her." Bleeding and hurt, she found herself outside, considerably hurt, in a field that had been recently plowed. It was quiet and a pale February sun was showing the time to be noon. By her sat a man, her love, who was crying. His crying was dampening the white shirt he wore and he used the damp cloth to wash her wounds, which were then healed. She looked at him to thank him, feeling the earth against her naked back, and he was lying on her without moving, feeling tremendously heavy. His weight was pushing her down, but underneath her the earth was pushing her up until she felt she *was* the earth itself. The man disappeared and she knew he was the sky and she the verdant earth beneath. "Thus they celebrated the marriage of heaven and earth. The union of the masculine and feminine principles" (Jacobi 1983).

Jacobi sent the dream to Jung in Zurich, and he replied that she was now "caught" and could not get away. She wrote back, asking if he would train her as an analyst, and he replied, only if she first got a doctorate. Perhaps he said this assuming that at her age, forty-four, she would not consider such a thing. But this was Jacobi, who, with her usual tremendous energy, enrolled in the University of Vienna and began to study psychology. Hitler's shadow was already spreading across Europe. Just four months before she was to get her degree, the Nazis marched into Vienna. Though a Jew, she had converted to Catholicism years before because of her attachment to a dying lover, but as a member of the Kulturbund she came under the scrutiny of the Gestapo and at one time they ransacked her apartment. She returned quickly to Budapest, where her husband, two sons, and her parents lived. From there she wrote to Jung, telling him what had happened in Vienna and asked if she could come to Zurich right away. He replied that no, she must first get her doctorate; this, in spite of the fact that many of the other women in his circle did not have degrees. It was a rather dangerous way to discourage her, if this was what was intended. And once more, he reckoned without her energy and resourcefulness. She returned to Vienna, fearing for her life, and stayed at the apartment of a friend, coming and going, veiled, as if in mourning. At forty-nine years old, she arrived in Zurich, degree in hand. Only one of her sons was able to get out of Hungary to join her. The other had to wait until the war was over. Her mother and father committed suicide, rather than go to the camps, and her husband died on his way to an internment camp.

Jacobi was born into a privileged, wealthy Jewish family in Budapest in 1890. Her father was a senator and a manufacturer. Both of her parents were Jewish, but both had been baptized Catholics. Anti-Semitism was all over Europe even then. When she was only nineteen, she married another wealthy man, Dr. Andreas Jacobi. She had two sons, but was restless just being a homemaker so she studied business so she might go to her husband's office and help. In 1919 there was a Communist takeover in Budapest and friends helped the family escape to Vienna. When the regime fell in 1925, her husband returned to Budapest, but left her and his sons behind for their education. Afterwards he divided his time between Budapest and Vienna. Jacobi came into her own with the Kulturbund and her prodigious energies.

Once in Zurich she had to begin her life all over again. She had a sharp tongue, about which Jung warned her in a letter dated 1941, only three years after her arrival. As the lone extravert, she was a natural impresaria, promoting Jung's work. As Dr. Joseph Henderson put it in an interview with me, "Sol Hurok Presents ... Jung" (Henderson 1977). And this was useful, if a bit unnerving for Jung and his close admirers.

In spite of all this, in her forty years as a Jungian analyst, she wrote several good books on Jung's psychology, which made much of his thought more accessible to the general public. Jung was both pleased and annoyed by this. Possibly Jung, who knew only too well how difficult his writing was for many people, was fearful of the popularization of his ideas and in his introversion was distrustful of her simplification and clarity.

In Jacobi's obituary, Baroness Vera von der Heydt wrote:

> When she presented him with *Psychological Reflections*, which is an anthology of Jung's ideas, as a gift for him on his seventieth birthday, his only comment was, "So you want people to read what you have put together instead of reading my books?" Jolande had obviously minded about the incident but was tough, and used to attacks and hostility and was smiling when she told me the story.
>
> *(Von der Heydt 1973)*

As irritated and jealous as he was of Jacobi, Jung realized she was an efficient extravert and great salesperson. Also she was a charming hostess. Much of the work she did for Jung, and later for his Institute, he simply could not have done alone. According to her detractors she was aggressive, pushy, and brassy, which is often how commanding women are judged. The rest of the Jungian women were all introverts and simply could not have done what she did.

When it became time for an Institute, it was to Jacobi that Jung turned. Actually she had put together some ideas for such an Institute several years before, but in 1948 she convinced Jung that if he was to have any control of such an institution he would have to organize it while he still lived. When he put her on the Curatorium, or Board of Governors, along with the only other woman, Liliane Frey-Rohn, there was much dissension, especially among the women. However, she did a great deal of good, as she was the only person who could put on a great front for the world. In the early days, she would greet the new students and visitors, and knew how to talk to them and how to present the new Institute.

She continued to have problems with the other women around Jung, not just because of her tongue, but because of their own jealousies and unwillingness to share him. Surprisingly, the only woman with whom she did not have a problem was Toni Wolff, who commanded her respect perhaps because she was a male-directed woman, too. When Toni died, Jacobi told Dr. Henderson, "She was like a rock. She could not be moved" (Henderson 1977).

Jacobi was as male-directed as many of the Jungian women were. In her work *Masks of the Soul*, cited in Claire Douglas' *The Woman in the Mirror*, "Women are viewed as complementary to men, women who pursue their own development are castigated for attempting to start an independent 'race of wonder women'" (Douglas 2000, p. 116). In a paragraph from that same book by Jacobi, she writes that in seeking self-development, women "forget that in doing so they deprive their husband of the chance to prove himself again and again as a man conquering and supporting her" (Jacobi 1976).

When Eranos got into full swing, especially after the Second World War, Jacobi had some problems with Erich Neumann, who was getting much attention and admiration from Jung for his work in analytical psychology. And Neumann sensed her hostility and felt his own toward her. He wrote in a letter to Jung, "I confess that I am naïve enough to consider Mrs. Jacobi's Catholicism as offensive" (Liebscher 2015, p. 239). Jacobi herself admitted that she sensed hostility from Jews because of her conversion, and from Catholics for the same reason. Attending Neumann's first lecture at Ascona in 1948 in which C. A. Meier, another Curatorium member, stormed out in the middle, Jacobi told Jung she felt Neumann was advocating a new dogmatism. Jung evidently did not agree. However, she and Meier continued to make things difficult for Neumann with the Zurich crowd, and as Fröbe-Kapteyn was an object of jealousy too, she and Neumann banded together as "outsiders."

We have a modern account from a present-day Jungian therapist and writer, Robert Johnson:

> I began analysis with Yolande [sic] Jacobi, who is probably the most unfortunate choice I could have made – I being an introverted feeling type and she being an extraverted Hungarian, who conducted her analytical hours pacing the floor, which always annoyed me. She told me that the apartment owner, next floor down, took her to court in Switzerland because she paced. The

Swiss judge heard her plea that, "I am Hungarian and I pace. That is part of my nature. It is my right to pace," and he said "All right, you may pace between 8 a.m. and 10 p.m., but not in the night."

(Segaller and Berger 1989)

She was an original, and like many such, full of contradictions. She has been called the "locomotive" and the "icebreaker," and some other nicknames unfit to print. She was also one of the clearest expositors of Jung's thought. Austria valued her services at the Kulturbund so highly, that in addition to the Knight's Cross of the Austrian Order of Service which she had been awarded in the 1930s, she was given honorary citizenship in 1957, something she prized very highly.

Jacobi died in 1973, just short of eighty-three years old.

References

Douglas, Claire (2000) *The Woman in the Mirror: Analytical Psychology and the Feminine.* Lincoln, Nebraska: iUniverse. First published Boston: Sigo Press, 1990.

Henderson, Joseph (November 1977) Author's interview.

Jacobi, Jolande (1976) *Masks of the Soul.* Grand Rapids, Michigan: Eerdmans.

Jacobi, Jolande (1983) *The Way of Individuation.* New York: New American Library.

Liebscher, Martin, ed. (2015) *Analytical Psychology in Exile: The Correspondence of C. G. Jung and Erich Neuman.* Philemon Foundation Series. Princeton, New Jersey and Oxford: Princeton University Press.

Segaller, Stephen and Berger, Merrill (1989) Robert Johnson interview. In *The Wisdom of the Dream, The World of C. G. Jung.* [Film.] London: RM Associates.

Von der Heydt, V. (1973) Obituary of Jolande Jacobi. *Quadrant.*

Wheelwright, Joseph (November 1977) Author's interview.

14

PRIESTESS

Dion Fortune

As the founder of the magical Society of the Inner Light, Dion Fortune might be considered an unlikely choice for this work. However, it was Jungian psychology and her friendship with Olga Fröbe-Kapteyn which had a great hand in the development of her thought and her life. Many of the other Jungian women either stayed close to Jung or visited him frequently as a way of renewing their links to him. Though she admired his work tremendously and found in his writings the intellectual basis for her life path, Dion Fortune never met Jung. She did, however, maintain a long correspondence with one of his closest associates, Olga Fröbe-Kapteyn, providing an important link to him as he was such a presence at the Eranos conferences from their inception in 1934. Fröbe-Kapteyn had taken the esoteric correspondence course that Fortune offered, and wrote that she would have liked to come to London, ostensibly to meet with Fortune, and that she was "working hard at the correspondences between Psychoanalysis, the Kaballah and ancient cults" (Hakl 2013, p. 333, n. 12).

At this point in the twentieth century, "The Jungian psychology was beginning to make an impact in esoteric circles, with its sympathy to mythology and even alchemy bringing, it was to be hoped, also a certain respectability and credibility to the occult" (Knight 2000, p. 217).

Little is known of the early life of this Englishwoman, born Violet Firth, other than her birthdate of December 6, 1896, in Wales. As many women of her time, she had little in the way of a classical education, but a very keen mind. She attended classes at the University of London and was most interested in classes given by a Professor Flugel, who, in addition to being a psychologist, was also President of the Society for Psychical Research. She was particularly interested in the work of Freud, Adler, and Jung. When later she worked in a clinic, she identified herself as a Freudian lay analyst. Gradually the tenets of Jung began to make more sense to her, especially with her growing interest in Eastern philosophies and magic. A friend of hers at the time reports it this way, "she saw quite exceptionally clearly the close connection between modern empiricism and tried and tested tenets of Tantric and Qabalistic ritualists … of the part played by the ancestral subconscious in the formation of character and personality" (Bernard Bromage, in *Light*, Spring 1960, quoted in Richardson 2000, pp. 52–53). Another source perhaps states it more clearly:

> [P]sychology was for Violet the Outer Court, as she would come to express it. It was her means of making magic acceptable to the world at large – it enabled her, she felt, to justify the philosophy and practice of magic, and to draw the right sort of (intelligent) people around the enchanted circle in which she found herself, outside of which she never stepped.
> *(Richardson 2000, p. 67)*

At this same time, she had a dream which changed the course of her life:

> [S]he saw herself reading in the library of the Theosophical Society headquarters in London. As she raised her eyes from her books, a section of the wall solid with books and shelves faded away revealing a stairway out into space.
> *(Fielding and Collins 1998, p. 20)*

She followed this stairway as the building disappeared, and finally came to a place where three great figures were standing. They were "a blend of columns of pulsating and moving force represented as colored lights and shaped into semblance of humanoid form" (Fielding and Collins 1998, p. 20). From her studies, she realized that one of them represented the forces of Nature, one the devotional path, and the other the hermetic or magical path. She was given to understand in the dream that hers was the hermetic path or path of the intellect, but she would need the balance of the other two in order to achieve her work. She was profoundly affected by this dream and made it the cornerstone of her life's task.

It was at this time that she "looked at my psychological work straight in the face and knew I could not longer go on with it, threw up my post and joined the ranks of the Land Army [those young women sent to replace, on farms, the men who left for war]" (Richardson 2000, p. 67). She had become aware in her practice that psychology did not have enough answers to satisfy her. This attitude may have been one of the reasons that prevented her from going to Jung and becoming one of the women in his circle. Another was the fact she was too much her own person to follow the tenets of another, even a genius. In any case, Jung would certainly have objected to her examining occultism in the light of psychology or vice versa. He took great pains for most of his career that no "taint" of occultism touch him and that his psychology be rooted in scientific thought. Two recent biographers, Colin Wilson and Gary Lachman, have taken him to task for this and have demonstrated clearly in their works the influence that paranormal experiences had on Jung's work and thought (Wilson 1984; Lachman 2010).

Dion Fortune's work, though expressed in a different language (magical as opposed to psychological), is clearly influenced by Jung.

> Dr. Jung has a great deal to say concerning the myth-making faculty of the human mind and the occultist knows it to be true. He knows also, however, that its implications are much further reaching than psychology has yet suspected.
>
> *(Dion Fortune, The Mystical Qabalah, quoted in Knight 2000, p. 218)*

According to one of her biographers, "Dion Fortune was always aware however that psychology was no substitute for occultism because it went nowhere deep enough" (Knight 2000, p. 218). An interesting bit of food for thought.

Her work in both fiction and non-fiction is concerned with the relationship between the sexes. "She felt as one of her tasks, the duty to put right the sexual interflow between man and woman not merely on the physical plane but on the inner planes as well" (Fielding and Collins 1998, p. 83). She frequently states in her work that the inner nature of woman is dynamic and the inner nature of man passive, and that on the inner planes it was the woman who activated the man. This sounds a bit like Jung's anima/animus theory, though a bit updated with a feminist perspective. This work became one of the great tasks for her magical master plan.

It is in her writings about the relationship between men and women that she seems most in harmony with the psychology of Jung, though her ideas in this respect were ahead of their time and perhaps even ours in this century, and ahead of Jung's ideas.

> There is a commonplace relationship which you can have with any female of the species, and there is a subtle, magnetic relationship.... People think that sex is physical and that love is emotional and they don't realize there is something else between a man and a woman which is magnetic in just the same way a compass turns to the Pole ... and it belongs to Nature.
>
> *(Fortune 2003, pp. 180–181)*

Throughout her work there are many parallels with Jung's ideas. *In Psychic Self-Defense*, for example, Fortune writes of

> the mind side of nature, invisible to our senses, intangible to our instruments of precision ... there are beings that live in this invisible world as fish live in the sea. There are also times when, as happens to a land when the sea dykes break, the invisible forces flow in upon us and swamp our lives.
>
> *(Fortune 1992, p. 23)*

This sounds very much like Jung's concept of the archetypes dwelling in the collective unconscious which can occasionally overcome us.

One can only wonder what might have happened if these two, Jung and Fortune, had actually met and whether there would have been any effect on Jung's work, especially as regards woman, the Feminine, and the anima. It is interesting to speculate that Jung, who was a voracious reader of English mysteries and who had been greatly impressed with H. Rider Haggard's book *She*, might have read one of Fortune's occult thrillers, such as *Moon Magic* or *Sea Priestess*, which were fictional accounts of her thought and magical practices, and an important aspect of her work.

When Dion founded the Society of the Inner Light, it was her goal, through magical practices, to bring the feminine back into balance with the masculine. In later times she harked back in her work to Arthurian and Grail themes. And after it was published, Jolande Jacobi's *The Psychology of C. G. Jung* was required reading for novices entering the Society, demonstrating she still felt the necessity for a psychological basis for magical work.

Fortune died in January 1946 at the age of fifty-five, after the rapid onset of a form of leukemia. She is buried in Glastonbury.

References

Fielding, Charles and Collins, Carr (1998) *The Story of Dion Fortune*. Loughborough, UK: Thoth Publications.
Fortune, Dion (1992) *Psychic Self Defense*. York Beach, Maine: Weiser Books.
Fortune, Dion (2003) *Priestess*. York Beach, Maine: Weiser Books.
Hakl, Hans Thomas (2013) *Eranos: An Alternative Intellectual History of the Twentieth Century*. Montreal: McGill-Queen's University Press.
Knight, Gareth (2000) *Dion Fortune and the Inner Light*. Loughborough, UK: Thoth Publications.
Lachman, Gary (2010) *Jung the Mystic*. New York: Jeremy Tarcher.
Richardson, Alan (2000) *Priestess*. Loughborough, UK: Thoth Publications.
Wilson, Colin (1984) *Lord of the Underworld: Jung and the Twentieth Century*. Wellingborough, UK: Aquarian Press.

15

THE VEILED LADY OF VISIONS
Christiana Morgan

In the last few years, the notes to Jung's seminars have finally been published. For a long time they were only available to students at the various C. G. Jung Institutes all over the world but now they've been edited and published for the general public. One of the most powerful of these documents is *The Visions Seminars*. And it masks perhaps the most tragic. The veil that the woman involved had purposely drawn was pulled aside and Christiana Morgan revealed.

The Visions Seminars is based entirely on the visions and drawings produced by Morgan during the course of her analysis with Jung in the 1920s using his technique of active imagination. She had taken to this process as a duck takes to water. As Claire Douglas has put it in her superb book on Morgan, "Christiana came up with unprecedented production of artistic and imaginative archetypal material" (Douglas 1993, p. 15). However, as she noted in her Introduction to the book, "Jung took Morgan's visions and imposed on them his own conceptual scheme ... Morgan herself vanished under the veil of his interpretation of her reality" (Douglas 1993, p. 15). And there will be more to say about this.

Morgan came from a patrician background and seemed to outwardly conform to the pattern of such women of her day – the party-going debutante, then respectable wife and mother. Her own private story was much more dramatic, including a teenage depression that required hospitalization. The prescription given at that hospital was typical of the times, and of the attitude toward women. She was to be kept still and inactive; she was to give up reading and using her mind.

She married a man just returned from the First World War, himself damaged, and she proceeded to do what many young women did. She tried living her life vicariously through his career, but he had little ambition and a much less forceful character than his wife. Inevitably, she turned to affairs with other men, until she encountered Harry Murray, her intellectual and passionate equal. Murray was married too, and the two couples, who were friends, struggled with the problem of the third couple of Harry and Christiana. Finally, Murray went to Zurich for analysis with Jung. Inevitably, Christiana followed.

Jung became enthralled with the amount and quality of visions produced by Morgan. Here was a non-psychotic woman producing a plethora of vividly colored symbolic material who was able to return after each vision to paint and write more. As it went on it was obvious that Jung was in the throes of a counter-transference. In this, he gave her the dubious advice to remain married while cultivating and developing her relationship with Murray. This was colored of course by his own situation, which he confided to her, of his relationship with Toni Wolff, in which he was currently involved. It was also colored by the nineteenth-century view of women, particularly acute in Switzerland. He advised her to be the muse or *femme inspiratrice* to Harry ... the same role assigned to Toni Wolff. As we have seen with Wolff, this was a role presenting many problems and sorrows for the woman playing it. In this way, Morgan's autonomous development was curtailed and put in service to the man in her life. This put Morgan on a path which she followed to the end of her life, costing her dearly.

A year after the end of Morgan's analysis, Jung wrote to her, telling her he was thinking of writing a book about her visions. She replied by sending her two journals containing all the drawings and notes.

In 1934, Jung held the "Visions" seminar. Afterward, a friend of Morgan's who attended shared its content with her. Although Jung did not reveal her name, many who attended made educated guesses and gossip spread quickly. Morgan was at this time involved with Murray in the running of a clinic they had set up in Boston and was very upset. She cabled Jung to stop the seminar, fearing the destruction of their present work. Jung did this, giving the "Nietzsche's *Zarathustra*" seminar instead.

Morgan continued her work and her life, experiencing the death of first her husband and then her father. But that life may have seemed rather pale after the excitement and passion of her days in Zurich with the charismatic Jung, and she experienced periodic depressive episodes the rest of her life.

In the end, she simply walked into the sea, that great and powerful image of the unconscious so often cited by Jung, and let herself drown. She was in her seventieth year and was survived by her true love, Harry Murray.

The story of Christiana Morgan was beautifully written in the biography by Claire Douglas. Interestingly, it was commented upon by a fourth-generation Jungian woman, Virginia Apperson, on the website of the C. G. Jung Society of Atlanta, Georgia. She quotes from the Introduction to Douglas' book:

> [I]nstead of cultivating their creativity for their own benefit, the women were encouraged to project onto a series of numinous men and to subordinate their own talents in order to advance the men's work.... Recently, some of these women – Lou Andreas-Salomé, Anaïs Nin, Ruth Mack Brunswick, Beata (Tala) Rank, Toni Wolff, Sabina Spielrein and Christiana Morgan – have

found a degree of recognition, but all lack a comprehensive and empathic analysis of their own struggle as creative women at the center of their own stories.

(Apperson, pp. 4–6)

She goes on to write, "if we expect Jung to have the final word then we deny our own daemonic potential whatever form it may take" (Apperson 2012). In 1974, I experienced a similar reminder while attending a conference hosting the American mythologist and author, Joseph Campbell. He gave a marvelous two-day series of lectures on the Hero's Journey, never using a note, which impressed me. At the end of the weekend, he asked for questions from the audience. I immediately raised my hand and was called on. I shared how much I'd enjoyed the lectures and then asked, "What was the woman's journey in all this?" Campbell gave an exaggerated sigh … then replied, "No woman has written of her journey, and until then we will not know."

I sat down rather stunned, while the rich collection of women who had done just that ran through my mind … Anaïs Nin, Colette, and several others. But then I realized there appeared to be little recognition of the woman's journey within a patriarchal system even by this man revered for his research on the mythical journeys of humanity across cultures and millennia. I continue to have hope this is changing, and it is.

References

Apperson, Virginia (2012) "My Break with Jung." C. G. Jung Society of Atlanta, *Newsletter* (Winter), pp. 4–6. www.jungatlanta.com/articles/winter12-my-break-with-jung.pdf.

Douglas, Claire (1993) *Translate this Darkness: The Life of Christiana Morgan, the Veiled Woman in Jung's Circle*. New York: Simon & Schuster.

16
THE REST OF THE ENTOURAGE

Barbara Hannah: daughter of the cathedral close

Hannah was born in 1891 in Brighton, England, where her father was Vicar of Brighton, then Dean of Chichester. A very sheltered beginning in the close of an Anglican cathedral where she lived her first forty years apart from two years spent studying art in Paris.

In all descriptions of her, she appears as the archetypal British spinster, much like a character in one of Agatha Christie's mystery novels, of which Jung was so fond. As a character, she stands out almost as much as Jacobi, though in a much different way. She stayed close to Jung and cold-shouldered others who wanted to get close to him. She was described by Mary Bancroft as

> a large English spinster of indeterminate age with a prominent nose that curved up to meet it [that] reminded me of the witch I had seen as a child in a production of *Hansel and Gretel* at the Boston Opera House. She was always making "in" jokes about arcane matters and laughing uproariously at certain obscure connections that puzzled me. She appeared oblivious of my existence and I felt that even to comment about something as harmless as the weather would only increase the desolation of Siberia to which she had apparently exiled me, thus defeating all attempts to establish contact.
>
> *(Bancroft 1975, p. 16)*

In 1928 after reading Jung's essay "Woman in Europe," Hannah went to Zurich to meet Jung. She was such an "animus hound [aggressive]" when she arrived that she regularly put people at a distance, other than Jung, upon whom she doted. She became known as Jung's greatest miracle. He managed to drive her energies into work, which then became analysis. Eventually she taught at the Institute.

Her original ambition had been to be a painter, so after reading Jung's essay she made up her mind to see him. She did a pencil sketch of him for his sixtieth birthday, but when some time later she asked him where it was, he confessed he didn't know. With this rejection from him she had no further desire to draw. When later she spoke of this to Jung, he felt that his forgetting was his unconscious way of leading her in a new direction, which became her writing.

Hannah wrote a number of books on analytical psychology. However, perhaps her most lasting claim to fame was her biography of Jung. At once chatty and informative, this is one of the more personal books about him, and in only a few places does it seem to smack of hero worship. But if she could be cloying, she also let some of Jung's less endearing ways be seen, subtly.

In her books on Jungian theory, "she continues the cultural restriction of women and feminine psychology to feelings, unconsciousness and relatedness.... In all her work, Hannah conserves Jung's original tendency to polarize what is appropriate to and characteristic of each sex" (Douglas 2000, p. 120). In this she was much like her lifetime roommate in Zurich, Marie-Louise von Franz.

Her works on the animus are much more helpful and show more regard for women. Claire Douglas has done a thorough examination of Hannah's work on this subject in her excellent book, *The Woman in the Mirror: Analytical Psychology and the Feminine* (Douglas 2000).

Hannah always felt she would live no longer than Jung's age at his death at eighty-five, which perhaps showed the depth of her dependency and attachment to him. However, she died in 1986 at the age of ninety-five.

Dr. Elizabeth Osterman: transformation[1]

In the late fall of 1977, I had the privilege of interviewing Dr. Osterman in her office in San Francisco. She was sixty-seven years old and one of the brightest and most interesting of all my interviews. Her educational background was formidable. She had received her master's degree in microbiology from the University of Washington, the state where she was born. Then she went on to Yale University to earn her doctorate in the same subject. She claimed she wanted to save the world, as in *Arrowsmith*, by conquering disease. But then she felt a pull toward something different and went to study at Stanford University, where she became a medical doctor. That still wasn't it, so she trained as a Jungian analyst at the San Francisco C. G. Jung Institute. She had decided she wanted to be helpful in a non-immediate, mothering way. A knowledgeable way.

> All my family thought I was strange. My sorority sisters thought I was strange. But I was an intuitive seeking time. My brother-in-law, who I think was envious, said I got a B.S. and then piled it higher. Then I did analysis with Dr. Elizabeth Whitney and I got down to where I was an egg … just a piece of protoplasm and that's all. I had to stop work. She found a home for me

with a friend of hers. She would come and visit me and we would talk. It was that going down into the dark … "I am an egg," I would say and she would say, "Oh, you're all right." And I was.

In the heat of my analysis, I had many dreams of going to Zurich – but inevitably the message came back. No! Your roots are here. Your tree grows here. In fact it was indicated that my leaves would be blighted if I went to Zurich. Of course the tree is one of my most vital images since I've been an adolescent.

Later on, my friend Maud Oakes, in the seventh year of my analysis, on the seventh day of the seventh month, suggested I go to Jung. So I went and I told him I had found my way to him almost like an accident. And he cured me of my European father complex in one afternoon. Ruth Bailey put two chairs by the Lake for us. As we sat down I looked at my watch. He said, "Never mind the time. I'll tell you when it's time to go." And we went back through time to pre-history. He told me, "You don't get rid of your complex, you drink it down to the dregs."

I came back to Zurich in time for the First International Congress. I was wandering around the Dolder Grand Hotel when Dr. Jacobi came up to me and said Jung wanted me to sit at his table that night. I went right out and bought pearls and white flowers. That night I sat at a marvelous round table that seated twelve, with Jung right there.

Being with Jung was like being more than yourself. It must have had an extraordinary effect on the women and I am wondering if they didn't have to become themselves *after* his death.

In my experience you meet the symbol representations, then meet them again higher on the spiral. What has been merely a bird in the tree becomes a marvelous visitation by the dove itself. I have finally found, at sixty-seven years old, that those things I am painting and dreaming for the last twenty-five years are now in my life. Where I was painting the sun rising up through the trees, now every morning of my life I wake up and see the sun rise through the trees.

The snake became the guardian of this house I found over five years ago in Mill Valley. I had had a dream two years before that there was a little wooden chapel in the woods. It had a Greek cross on the end of the gable. After I moved into it the neighbor who knew the history of the house said, "Oh this used to be the little chapel." The first day I was there I saw a snake. It went off into a dark corner. My helper was in another room, and I thought, "If she knows this, she'll never come back." So I closed the door. In the process of getting it out, I wounded it mortally and I felt just dreadful. I thought I had to do something. It was one of those nights when the moon comes up on one side while the sun goes down on the other. So I went in the back where the pine trees are and I dug a hole. I put a candle on one side and some water on the other. And a blue stone of healing on one side and the black one – obsidian – on the other and the snake in the hole just as the sun went down and the moon went up. I said, "Please forgive me. I didn't mean to harm you." And just like that, I had the feeling that the spirit of the snake had become the soul of the house. After that I had carpenters do some work on the house. Six weeks later, I came in with my suitcases, walked out onto the deck. Though the deck was fifteen feet off the ground, I saw what I had never seen before or since: the full shed skin of a snake. The molting had occurred – the transformation had taken place.

We talked for a while longer, and she added two ideas. "Your book must have the unconscious in it as that was what Jung was about." And when I had given a quick vignette about my experience in Brazil, she said, "If your path led through the Goddess then you are halfway there. Because you've gone deeply into the primordial."

Then I took my leave. I never saw her again, but read her obituary on July 8, 1998. It said she often said the latter years of her old age were the happiest of her life. And I believe that, living as she did her Jungian precepts.

Dora Kalff: sand dreams

One of the finest techniques to emerge from analytical psychology, in my estimation, has been Sandplay Therapy, as developed and created by Dora Kalff.

Kalff was a divorced single mother of two sons and the story goes she was living in the mountains of Switzerland, where Jung's daughter Gret was spending the summer with her children. Gret noticed that whenever her children would visit with Kalff and her family they would come back unusually content. Jung's daughter met Kalff and spoke with her, and encouraged her to study psychology and to speak with her father, C. G. Jung. Kalff did just that, and was encouraged by him to further her studies in London with Margaret Lowenfeld, who was famous for her World Technique of play therapy with children. Kalff went to London and saw immediately that the sandboxes where Lowenfeld allowed the children to express themselves were also a way to access the unconscious mind and dream state. After a year with her, Kalff returned to Zurich and with Lowenfeld's permission, combined the World Technique with Jungian psychology. The result was Sandplay Therapy, used all over the world for both adults and children.

Kalff herself lived in a house in nearby Zollikon, about which she wrote, "My house was constructed hundreds of years ago on rock; its rooms were not built and shaped with yardstick and compass, but grew according to natural law" (Kalff 1980). And I experienced the truth of this when I studied with her there, many years ago.

During the exodus of so many Tibetans due to the takeover by Communist China and the resulting intolerance of their Tibetan Buddhist religion, many found their way to Switzerland, including one monk whom Kalff was asked to let live in her home for a week. His name was Geshe Chodrak, from the Sera Monastery in Tibet. He stayed eight years, and since he was the soothsayer of His Holiness the Dalai Lama, that august person visited frequently. Kalff had many sessions with him.

84 The rest of the entourage

As a result, Dora Kalff became a practitioner of Tibetan Buddhism while remaining a Catholic. She began to see her Sandplay sessions as a form of sitting meditation, which enables the therapist to go within and create calm. She also began to view the therapist as a "witness" rather than an authority figure. Later, Kalff would teach her students: "This work is about being a spiritual therapist" (Kalff 1980). And her house reflected this in its display of many thangkas and other assorted Tibetan art work. It seemed a natural setting for it. Later she was instrumental in obtaining the house next door to hers as a center for the local Tibetan population.

In one of her audiences with the Dalai Lama, "His Holiness asked Kalff 'how she could recognize in the sand whether someone had been living on a different planet in previous lifetimes, and what symbols would point to that,'" recalls her son Martin. "She, of course, was not able to answer ... all these encounters gave her courage to do her work and trust in the deeper aspects of the psyche" (Chang 2003).

Because Kalff herself was a polyglot, speaking German, Italian, French, English, and Dutch, she was able to teach her technique to other Jungian analysts all over the world. In addition to studying with her in Zollikon while I was at the C. G. Jung Institute in Zurich, I studied further with her at a long seminar she held at the University of California, Santa Cruz a few years later. Working with her was a marvelous experience. I saw instantly the language of dreams and fantasy played out in the sandboxes, which were made of specific dimensions, containing the miniature figures chosen and placed by her clients in session.

Frau Kalff taught her technique right up to a few months before she died at the age of eighty-six at her home in Zollikon. The home built on rock.

Mary Foote's notes[2]

Amazingly, transcripts of Jung's seminars had been unavailable to the general public until only recently – Jung never wrote them down himself – and only after they were painstakingly transcribed over many years by Mary Foote. Foote's own story is worth a book in itself, though as of now I know of no such book.

Orphaned at an early age, she was taken in by relatives and the next we hear of her, she was a portrait painter of some note after having studied at Yale and in Paris with John Singer Sargent and others. In her studio at Number 3, Washington Square in New York City, she brought together some of the brightest lights of the art and entertainment world. Robert Edmund Jones, the set designer, was a close friend. It was in his letters from Zurich, where he had gone to have analysis with Jung, that she first heard of that great man. The letters were instrumental in bringing her to Zurich many years later. Another close friend was Mabel Dodge Luhan, living in Taos, New Mexico, herself a painter and an author. Other close friends were D. H. Lawrence, and Henry James. In childhood, Foote had met and known Mark Twain.

A great deal of the information we have about Foote's years in Zurich comes from her correspondence with Luhan. However, before landing in Zurich, she first went to Peking, China, sailing from New York in Christmas of 1926. It was in

Peking where a traumatic event occurred that caused her to write to Jung. His reply suggests that she had asked if it were any use to go into analysis at fifty-four years old. "Dear Miss Foote, I rather prefer to have you come to Zurich about the middle of October [1927] for the Winter term. Age is of no importance. As long as you live, you have the problems of the living, only different ones than at 20. Sincerely yours, C. G. Jung" (Foote 1971).

For an idea of the trauma that led Foote to write to Jung, we read in the memoir by Mary Bancroft that author Ann Bridge had put Foote in a novel called *Peking Picnic*, and the shock of seeing herself portrayed as she had never seen herself had caused Foote to come to Zurich to see Jung. "I was told in this connection that a 'sudden confrontation with the shadow' could be devastating" (Bancroft 1975, p. 117).

Foote arrived in Switzerland after traveling across China on the Trans-Siberian Express, then the Orient Express, to Marseilles. She arrived in Zurich in July, 1927. Her stay was only brief, but she returned in January 1928, remaining there for the next twenty-five years.

In one of her letters to Luhan, Foote writes: "Jung doesn't remove complexes and he thinks all progress comes from conflict so, I suppose, one will go on conflicting for the rest of one's life." In this she sounds weary and discouraged, most probably because she was far from home, hard at work in unfamiliar surroundings. She never returned home until she was in her nineties.

As a foreign visitor, Foote found the conditions challenging.

> It's no use unless you can face considerable difficulty of one kind or another. In the first place the isolation and gray damp weather of Zurich and the amount of time it takes to batter through at our age and the probability of a not-particularly-thrilling collection of people to play with.

She goes on to warn Luhan, to whom she is writing, that she might not like the humble conditions. Much of the letter is an exaggeration, perhaps to keep Luhan from coming to Zurich. Much of what Foote says is true for the solitary tourist. "I wake up with the horrors frequently, but it isn't as bad as when I was trying to pay my way in New York."

The next letter gives an indication of what was to keep her in Zurich the rest of her active life.

> There are a few people here whom I like, but I am living the most utterly monastic life, sitting in the same spot day after day.... I am interested and working hard ... not much painting now – but doing some writing, ARRANGING NOTES FOR JUNG not original or to be published or anything, but exceedingly instructive and good for me.

These "nothing important" notes were to become some of the most important work done for Jung, becoming transcripts of the seminars on Analytical Psychology, conducted by Jung for his English-speaking students, patients, and colleagues from 1929 to 1939. Without them, the seminars would have been lost and unavailable to succeeding generations of students at the Institutes, and now, the world at large. They are exceedingly useful in the interpretation of symbolic material.

Mary Foote paid out of her own pocket, limited though it was, to have these notes copied and sent to subscribers throughout the world. There were never more than a hundred subscribers, so the cost of printing and mailing was paid by her. Again, Jung was to receive much in return from a woman who admired him. Mary Foote was able to work closely with Jung as he went over the notes, and perhaps felt it was well worth the cost to her.

Even when the seminars were discontinued because of the war, she made it her life work to edit them and eliminate all errors, continuing to do this into her old age. In the 1950s, Foote became ill with dementia. Another American woman analyst, Mary Briner, brought her home to America, where she died in a Connecticut nursing home in 1968 at the age of ninety-six.

Mary Bancroft: the spy who loved him

When she left America and went to Zurich to live with her businessman husband, one of the first things Mary Bancroft did was go to a series of lectures Jung was giving at the Eidengenossische Hochschule to see who he was before she made a commitment to analysis. She had unfortunate sneezing fits at the most embarrassing times and wanted to see what was causing them.

> I do remember how tremendously impressed I was by him. Although he was twenty-eight years older than I, I found him extremely attractive as a man. This was a shock. Until that moment I had never regarded men more than at most ten years older than myself as "sex objects." But what impressed me was his perfectly extraordinary wit, so rare in a person of his vast erudition.
>
> *(Bancroft 1975, p. 115)*

Next, she went to the English Seminars at the Psychological Club, followed by a tricky analysis with Toni Wolff. Tricky, because their personalities seemed to clash, and she was relieved when she had a dream that Wolff said indicated she should have analysis with Jung, which she did, for four years. During that time, she was recruited by Allen Dulles, who also became her lover, to spy for the OSS (Office of Strategic Services, US wartime intelligence service) as the Second World War was beginning. Dulles had slipped into Switzerland just ahead of the Nazi march into France. The borders were then sealed. Unable to bring any of his usual OSS officers into the country, he recruited people he met in Zurich for different tasks. Bancroft's biggest worry, which she shared in analysis with Jung, was whether she could keep her mouth shut as she was such an extravert. He said he thought she could do it, but added, "Probably only the thought that five thousand people would be dead if you didn't would ever make you do it." He also told her doing such a job would probably reveal to her much more about herself, which she subsequently found to be true.

Possibly the secret she had to keep to herself that was the most dangerous was the fact there was a conspiracy against Hitler by his officers, generals, and some highly placed German citizens. The fact that Jung was also in on the information with Dulles' knowledge should stop once and for all the persistent rumors that Jung was a Nazi sympathizer. Dulles would never have confided in him if that had been the case.

Bancroft came from a wealthy, prominent American family, and was born in Boston in 1903. Her family published the *Wall Street Journal*. It was after her second marriage to a Swiss banker that she moved to Zurich, where her husband had his business. She was beautiful, sexy, intelligent, and very vivacious and interested in everything. Jung told her in the course of her analysis that "As an extraverted intuitive, power is your natural element. Men seeking or holding power will seek your advice" (Bancroft 1997, p. 61). When she told him in the course of their meetings that Dulles had given her the use of his car, "he said that men like Dulles, very ambitious and holding positions of power, needed to listen to what women were saying in order to exercise their best judgment and not go off the deep end" (Bancroft 1983).

Also in analysis she was at last able to relieve herself of her sneezing fits when she realized they were a reaction to a feeling she couldn't say "no" to anyone for fear they wouldn't love her. With Jung's help, she also rid herself of a writing block, a serious difficulty for she was also a journalist.

Bancroft stayed on in Zurich until after the end of the Second World War, staying in constant touch with Jung. Eventually she moved to New York and became a staunch supporter of the C. G. Jung Institute there.

Writing Jung that she understood that in some tribes the chief would answer one question from each of his followers on his eightieth birthday, and since it was his, she asked "Have you ever seen a helpless woman, as I never have." His answer was that a man's helplessness can be real, but "a woman's is one of her best stunts. As she is by birth and sex on better terms with Nature, she is never quite helpless as long as there is no man in the vicinity."

Mary Bancroft died at ninety-three.

Hilde Kirsch: the exile[3]

Hilde Kirsch was born into a wealthy Jewish family in Germany and led an enviable life until her father died and things became more difficult. She married and had two children, but her husband died from a fatal disease, leaving her with the children. Shortly afterward, Hitler rose to power and she knew she must leave and take her children to Palestine, which she did in 1935. Once there, she wrote to Jung asking if she might have therapy with him that spring. He replied that he was much too busy and she would have to wait for a year. With such tragedy behind her, she felt that a year was too much to wait and so she sat down and consulted the *I Ching*, for the first time in her life. It advised her in the Changing Line that she should "cross the water to see the Great Man." Despite the Nazi threat in Europe, she took the next boat for Europe.

As Fate would have it, when in Zurich she moved into a *pension* and met a woman there who was having an analysis with Jung. The morning after her arrival, the woman summoned Hilde to her room and asked her the favor of telephoning Jung to tell him she was too ill to come to her appointment that morning and to cancel. Happily, Hilde did as requested, asking firmly to speak to Jung himself, though he did not like using the telephone. She gave him the woman's message, told him who she was and that the *I Ching* had told her to come and she wanted the appointment that had just become available. He roared with laughter and told her to come. Once there, she found he had been telling the truth in his letter and he was booked all day long. Hilde had to come at seven o'clock in the morning for all future appointments.

Her analysis with Jung was so life-changing that she felt impelled to become an analyst herself and share his method with the world. She studied in Zurich, then met and married another German refugee and analyst, Dr. James Kirsch. Together with her children, they left for England. In London they were part of a group that formed the Medical Society for Jungian Psychology. However, as Hitler came closer and France fell, America seemed the only safe choice. They had survived a hundred air raids in London and then had to journey by ship through waters infested with U-boats to get there but it did not seem any more dangerous than what they had already experienced. Once in America they settled in Los Angeles, where they founded the C. G. Jung Analytical Psychology Club, and later the C. G. Jung Institute.

It was fourteen years later that she once again returned to Zurich to see Jung. When she entered his consulting room, she looked around at all the things that had been there when she first saw him. As if he read her thoughts, he said, "Yes, Hilde. Everything is just the same." When she sat down, he picked up with the dream she had when she last saw him, fourteen years and a world war before. Having had her world turned upside down several times and needing a feeling of continuity, Jung provided it in a simple, caring way. Reassurance on a deep level.

Then she spoke of a dream she had that was embarrassing to her, in which she had been his bride. He replied that the dream was true symbolically, as she was a Taurus and he had his Moon in Taurus, which matched them astrologically. Her embarrassment was eased and she felt healed by his response. Jung often was careful with the feelings of the women, conscious of the effect he had on them.

After forty years as a lay analyst, Hilde Kirsch's career ended with her death in 1978, shortly after our interview. The Hilde Kirsch Children's Center at the C. G. Jung Institute of Los Angeles is named after her.

Lucile Elliott: the dreamer[4]

Like many of the early followers of Jung, Elliott began her career as a medical doctor, graduating with a medical degree from the University of California in 1924. This was after the suffragettes had won the right to vote for women, and she found her medical school to be without prejudice against female students. Internships were granted based on grades, regardless of whether one was male or female. She began her career in Berkeley, California.

However, a few years into that career, she found herself in "an intolerable situation which I couldn't take and couldn't leave alone." She sought help from Dr. Elizabeth Whitney, one of the first Jungian analysts in the San Francisco Bay Area. Five years later, still in analysis, she felt she needed something else and Dr. Whitney sent her to Zurich, to Dr. Jung, in 1935.

"He was the greatest man I ever met." And she had a six-month analysis with him, feeling healed. Other than for analysis, she stayed most of the time in her hotel room, meeting no one but Barbara Hannah, who was living in the same hotel. "When she [Hannah] entered the room, it was as if a dark shadow entered" – much the same experience as shared by other women close to Jung.

Once back in San Francisco, she felt healed enough that she no longer pursued analysis, but did not feel ready to be an analyst herself. A few years later, Dr. Joseph Wheelwright and his wife, Jane, newly returned from Zurich, together with Elizabeth Whitney and Elliott formed the Society of Jungian Analysts of San Francisco. Just a year or so later, the Second World War broke out and once more Elliott had to postpone becoming an analyst as so many doctors were being called into the military that there was a danger of a shortage of doctors for the civilian population. Finally, in 1946, the war over, Dr. Elliott gave up general medicine and became an analyst. She continued practicing analysis until her eyesight began to fail in her later eighties, and a bad knee forced her to live in a retirement home. All the wisdom of her rich life was in her face when I interviewed her, continually crinkling into good humor.

Then she said, "Jung really hurt my feelings." It seemed she had gone to Zurich a second time, having lost someone with whom she had a twenty-six-year relationship. He had died, and she had a disturbing dream in which she had been lying in a coffin near his grave and a tree was growing out of her forehead. In the dream she kept getting out of her coffin to go to her friend's grave. She had been profoundly disturbed by the dream, thinking maybe it was a desire to die, or maybe a sign of new life. Because he had helped her so much before, she went back to Zurich to see Jung. He refused to see her, saying she was still too involved with him and he was now too old to work it through with her. He was almost eighty. So instead, she had an hour with Emma Jung, who was kind and helpful, but the refusal of Jung to see her stayed with her even as she recounted the story.

When I asked if it still hurt, she said:

> Oh, a few years ago I had a vision of Dr. Jung rising from the depths of the water. He had a black veil over him, covered with jewels all over. He had his same friendly smile, but now his hair was long and I could see that he looked like an Old Testament prophet. That healed the hurt.

And I wonder, "The Old Testament prophet, Elijah?"

Notes

1 This section is based on the personal recorded interview by the author of Dr. Elizabeth Osterman in her San Francisco office in fall 1977.
2 Much of the material in this section is from personal interviews by the author and from Foote 1971.
3 This section is based on the personal interview by the author of Mrs. Kirsch in her Los Angeles home in February 1978, shortly before her death.
4 This section is based on the personal interview by the author of Dr. Elliott in her San Francisco Bay Area retirement home in February 1978.

References

Bancroft, Mary (1975) "Jung and His Circle." *Psychological Perspectives: A Quarterly Journal of Jungian Thought* 6(2): 114–127.
Bancroft, Mary (1983) *Autobiography of a Spy.* New York: Wm. Morrow & Co.
Bancroft, Mary (1997) *Mary Bancroft Memorial Issue. Spring: A Journal of Archetype and Culture*: 6.
Chang, Helen (2003) "Dora Kalff's Life." *Mandala Quarterly* [Portland, Oregon: FPMT] (June).
Douglas, Claire (2000) *The Woman in the Mirror: Analytical Psychology and the Feminine.* Lincoln, Nebraska: iUniverse. First published Boston: Sigo Press, 1990.
Foote, Edward (1971) "Who Was Mary Foote?" *Spring: A Journal of Archetype and Culture*: 256–268.
Kalff, Dora M. (1980) *Sandplay: A Psychotherapeutic Approach to the Psyche.* Boston: Sigo Press.

17

JUNG

The *animus mundi*

Why is it so many strong, intelligent, and mostly well-educated women flocked to Jung? This is a question asked by many people. And my answer is simple: revolution! The early years of the twentieth century were revolutionary … politically, intellectually, artistically, and women in many countries were organizing to get more of a say in how their governments were run. Psychoanalysis itself was revolutionary: "the talking cure." Instead of simply receiving treatment for their symptoms, and mostly these "treatments" did not work, the mentally disturbed were being listened to for perhaps the first time ever. In the forefront of this movement, there were two figures who stood out: Freud and Jung. And it was noticeable early on that most of the followers of Jung, who came to "talk" and stayed to do the work themselves and be close to him, were women. He was a charismatic figure, it was recognized early, full of health and vitality, recognizable as a healer or shamanic man. He was also a very complex man, full of contradictions and unconscious attitudes that were to color his psychological concepts.

Throughout this book some of his unconscious attitudes regarding women, and the feminine in general, have been noted. They were attitudes about women common to the patriarchal system of his day, and, some might venture to say, the last 2,000 years. Not just attitudes, but accepted views of the Church and the State. And they were common to the men who were in positions of power within those institutions. So it is not surprising that when these attitudes were demonstrated in statements by Jung, the women themselves took them as given, despite their intelligence and vague inner knowing.

Some of the women, in particular Barbara Hannah, said they were first attracted to Jung by a magazine article he wrote, "Woman in Europe," which contained many of the sentiments of the day. "It is a woman's outstanding characteristic that she can do anything for the love of a man. But those women who can achieve something important for the love of a thing are most exceptional…. Love for a thing is a man's prerogative." And, "Unconscious assumptions or opinions are the worst enemy of woman; they can even grow into a positively demonic passion that exasperates and disgusts men, and does the woman herself the greatest injury." However, possibly it was just the idea he would write about women at all that was the draw.

Another draw was possibly the women sensing that Jung needed them as much as they needed him. In *Aion*, written in 1951, as referenced by Paul Bishop, Jung asserts, "that the Anima is related to the image of Mother and 'every mother and beloved is the carrier and embodiment of this dangerous mirage, which corresponds to the deepest reality in a man'" (Bishop 1995, pp. 201–202). In his own personal psychology, given the early absence of his mother and the substitution of a young maid in the household, this probably intensified the "dangerous" aspect of this projection. Emma Jung and Toni Wolff (and, to some extent, Sabina Spielrein) played out these unconscious roles in his personal life. I have shown how his relationship to his mother, Emilie Preiswerk Jung, laid the basis for his relationship to women in general, and to those in his circle in particular. It created within him a lifelong need for the creative and intellectual companionship of women. The need seems of a size proportionate to his gifts, and was not simply the desire of most men to be admired by women, although that was certainly present. In *The Red Book*, one of the first of his visions contained a very powerful woman, Salome.

Even in a near-death experience he described, it was Jung's connection to the women that had a great deal to do with his survival. In the midst of it, the doctor who had been treating him floated to him in a vision. The phantom doctor explained to Jung that he wasn't allowed to die because at least thirty women were too upset at the idea of his leaving them and his work.

Jung's was a deep psychic need on which his creativity and the wholeness of his psyche were dependent. His awareness of this, even unconsciously, was what possibly gave him his ambivalent feelings about them. After all, he chose a woman not his wife, Toni Wolff, to accompany him on his journey into his own unconscious mind, and who thus became Jung's analyst. For him, women and the unconscious were virtually synonymous. He had said that if men made an infantile resistance to women, they were also resisting their own unconscious side.

In spite of his psychological theories and public statements, particularly in many of his writings, Jung took women very seriously, which is something that came across repeatedly in the women whom I was able to interview. One pointed out to me that Jung's typology is non-sexist and helped women out of their Victorian prison. However, another Jungian wrote: "He seemed surprised that women should think rather than feel, and work rather than mother" (Samuels 1986, p. 215). And, "For instance in his general description of the various psychological types, Jung claims that introverted feeling is mainly to be found among women" (Samuels 1986, p. 215). This writer then goes on to make the point, which is one I would like to emphasize:

> I am not alone in being struck by the discrepancies between these attitudes of Jung's … on the one hand, and on the other, the life in Zurich between the

wars. In the sub-culture of analytical psychology at least, the city was home to several high-achieving women analysts. These women … do not appear to have felt any anxiety or conflict between their career orientation and what they had to say about being feminine.

(Samuels 1986, p. 215)

The women who came to Jung seemed to thrive on whatever it was that he gave them in analysis and relationship. The exact nature of what that was varied from person to person. Part of it came certainly from their projections onto him of the genuine wise man, teacher, and shaman. However, it is documented by several of the women that he gave these projections back to the women for them to integrate into their own psyches. If he had not, they would never have been able to write their books, teach their classes, or give analytical hours. Repeatedly I was quoted the dreams of the women in my interviews with them, in which they told me of ways Jung had been seen in those dreams and when they spoke of these images in analysis, he explained that those were projections onto him of what existed in the women themselves.

It is important also to realize what these women had in common. Many of the women who came to him, such as Bertine, Harding, Mann, and others, were already professionals. But this was a lonely way for a woman in the first decades of the twentieth century. Many others had simply stifled their ambitions and channeled them into possibly inappropriate but socially acceptable areas. We still see today women who drive their husbands and children to hypertension with their own swallowed ambitions, often turned aggressive. If there are no families in whom they can live out their drives, often this goes into negative relationships. Most of the women came to Jung with neuroses, and to what extent this was because of swallowed ambitions can only be guessed. It is possible that whatever problems they had were made worse by a lack of outlets for their enormous energies and talents.

Some had university training and others little or no formal education, which was not unusual for women at that time. However, most came from cultured backgrounds and were mostly upper class, no matter their countries of origin. This is easily conjectured by the fact that only the upper classes and intelligentsia traveled in those days. It is only in the last sixty or seventy years that foreign travel, other than for immigration or military purposes, has spread to the general public.

One of the Jungian women, not in the inner circle, pointed out to me that all these women had big animuses. Animus is a term used (confusedly at times) by Jungians to explain the more aggressive or assertive characteristics in women. These are attributed to an inner masculine image. However, this term had much to do with what society did and did not feel were a woman's natural instincts. Jung, instead of merely describing them as "unfeminine" traits, gave them a catch-all word: animus. He stated there were positive and negative aspects to the animus, but more often seemed to regard it with fear and loathing. "A woman should constantly control the animus: by undertaking some intellectual work, many a woman has been driven to disaster by her animus." And "If a woman dreams of a superior role she wishes to assume in the world, it is best to advise her to write an essay or an article about her wishes" (Samuels 1986, p. 216). As a way of not trying to fulfill her wishes, and sublimating instead, one wonders? In any case, some of the Jungian women, such as author and analyst Irene Claremont de Castillejo and even Emma Jung in her essay on the animus, tried to enlarge and clarify, in a woman's terms, the positive aspects of this archetype (Castillejo 1973; Jung, E. 1985). According to one woman analyst:

> With Jung, for the first time the animus had a place to go so he attracted all these women with whopping great animuses and the rest wound up in booby hatches. In my day it was "never let the animus out when a man is around."
> *(Ostrowski-Sachs 1977)*

Jung seemed to have an uncanny knack of seeing – in each woman who came to him – her true gifts and talents and an even more useful knack of evoking these gifts. Even putting them to his own use, as seen with Marie-Louise von Franz, and others. This process smacks of an old ceremonial magic technique, used by secret lodges and societies, particularly in the late nineteenth through twentieth centuries, of creating a magical image. Dion Fortune gives a good description of this in one of her popular magic novels. It is a dialogue between a man and the woman who is in the process of becoming a priestess of the Sea Goddess in the twentieth century:

> "The next step," said she, staring into the fires and not looking at me, "is to complete my own training."
> "That being?" said I.
> "To make the magical image of myself as a sea priestess. A magical image does not exist on this plane at all. It is in another dimension, and we make it with the imagination. As for that, I cannot do it alone. For me to make a magical image of myself is auto-suggestion and this begins and ends subjectively. But when two or three of us work together, and you picture me as I picture myself, then things begin to happen."
> *(Fortune 2003, p. 51)*

I have quoted verbatim because I believe it describes the Dionysian initiation or calling out of woman. Jung saw something in these women in analysis that they did not see or dare to express in everyday life until he saw it and called it out. Women were not supposed to have ambitions or talents to make a serious contribution. Dionysus was the God of Arrival, and His arrival called women out of their homes where they had been stuck and called them to play and to ritual. Author and Jung biographer Paul Bishop has written of psychoanalyst John Gedo and sociologist Peter Homans, who

> argue that Jung saw himself as a prophetic figure "in the midst of the terrible chill, a solitary leaf bearing but fruitless tree remains ... my tree of life," Jung

remarks, whose leaves are transformed by the effects of the frost into sweet grapes of healing which Jung plucks and distributes to a large waiting crowd.

If, in his letter to Freud, Jung had expressed the wish "to transform Christ back into the soothsaying god of the vine, which he was," in this dream Jung himself actually *becomes* the divine Dionysus.

(Bishop 2014, p. 119)

And of course, in the Introduction to Linda Fierz-David's book on the mysteries of Dionysus, Jung refers to her as "my Ariadne."

This might be one of the reasons the first generation of women around Jung so jealously guarded their space. By guarding it so assiduously from newcomers until they could prove themselves permanent, they were making it a safe place. There were not many such places for intellectual women outside the universities, and often women were not welcome there.

Jung also fulfilled another role, that of shaman, or medicine man of his "tribe." Being a shaman is different from being a priest. A priest is always tied to the society in which he lives or the church which he serves. In delivering the words of the gods or the unconscious, he also gives those of society and its expectations. He is almost always seen as the intermediary between gods and humankind. The shaman is the loner, the one who seeks out his own way in the wilderness of the human condition, and takes no one else's or no institution's word for what the gods say. If he has followers, he passes on the spiritual truths he or she has learned from his/her own experience, but encourages them to have their own experiences of the Divine. In Joseph Campbell's words, "the shaman is one, who, as a consequence of personal psychological crisis, thus has gained a certain power of his own" (Campbell 2002, p. 166). Jung's plunge into his own psyche, as revealed in *The Red Book*, certainly gave him an authority no amount of education could have provided.

Dr. Joseph Henderson spoke of the uncanny side of Jung's nature, which at times made him seem almost frightening. He described it as Jung's shamanistic side, which endowed him with a kind of intuition that could go right to the heart of a person's troubles with great perception (Henderson 1977). He had an uncanny way of coming right to the heart of something without consciously knowing what was wrong. One doctor whom I interviewed even spoke of Jung being unconscious and operating from that level.

Jung himself describes how he was asked by another doctor to see a young woman whom the doctor had not been able to help and who was, seemingly, beyond help. The woman showed up as arranged, to see Jung, and he spent an hour with her. During this time an old nursery rhyme came into his head, and he began to sing it. The hour soon came to an end and she left. He did not hear anything more of her or her case until years later when the same doctor whom he had seen years before came over to him. He asked Jung what "miracle" he had performed, for she had come home completely cured and even now was living a normal life (Jaffé 1989, p. 132).

Dr. Heinrich Fierz told me several similar stories of Jung's ability to just make a simple gesture which seemed to heal … like the slow wave of his hand at a Psychological Club meeting where certain members had begun a heated argument, then fell silent at the gesture.

Over and over again we have stories of Jung's ability to "read minds" as he did to reassure Hilde Kirsch when she returned after a long absence to see him. Renée Brand told a story if how she and ten students from the Institute were invited to the planting of a tree at Jung's home on his eightieth birthday. She noticed how frail he was, and as gardeners were digging a hole for the tree, she began to have an awareness of a more sinister implication for the hole. Suddenly Jung was beside her telling her it was not a burial but the planting of new life.

Another author writes: "The main talent of the shaman is throwing himself into a trance at will … and it is while he is in this trance that he performs his miraculous deeds" (Campbell 2002, p. 166).

Because of this ability to virtually mind-read, he met his patients at a very deep level. And it is no wonder that the women spoke of "miracles" at times. In a world where there is so much talk about communication but where there is still so very little true communication, to be met at this level and by someone who answers questions without one ever needing to ask them does seem miraculous.

> The shaman … is not only a familiar denizen, but even a favored scion, of those realms of power that are invisible to our normal waking consciousness, which all may visit briefly in vision, but through which he roams as a master.
> *(Campbell 2002, p. 166)*

And another common view of Jung is that of the Wise Old Man of Bollingen Tower. When his name is mentioned now, the picture it evokes is that of the white-haired old man of later years. As Barbara Hannah wrote in her biography of Jung, "his school fellows at the gymnasium already called him 'Father Abraham'" (Hannah 1976, p. 53). From an early age he had seemed too old for his years and while still a child was aware of himself as an old man. He writes of how, at twelve years old, he frightened his host by standing up in the back of a boat, for which he received a dressing-down.

> I was thoroughly crestfallen and had to admit I had done exactly what he had asked me not to do, and that his rage was quite justified. At the same time I was seized with a rage that this fat, ignorant boor should dare to insult ME.
> *(Jung 1965, p. 33)*

He goes on to describe the second personality of which he became aware while still a child. This second personality was an older, distinguished man, an important man, whom Jung felt inside himself. This personality seemed to emerge in times of stress or confrontation.

This aspect of Jung was particularly noticeable with those who met him in his later years. In her interview, Elizabeth Osterman told me that the force that came from him was incredible, that he seemed very aware of this power, although in no way would he misuse it (Osterman 1977).

Perhaps it was this part of his psyche that he did not become fully aware of until he went into his dark night of the soul and began to have the visions which went into *The Red Book*. The first character in those visions was Elijah. He described how the scene was that of an ultimate reality where he saw the white-bearded old prophet, accompanied by a young beautiful woman who was introduced as Salome. From the figure of Elijah in this fantasy came another, Philemon. Philemon appeared to him as a "winged being sailing across the sky. I saw he was an old man with the horns of a bull. He held a bunch of four keys … he had the wings of a kingfisher with its characteristic colors" (Jung 1965, p. 33).

Much later he was able to say, "At Bollingen I am in the midst of my true life" (Jung 1965, p. 181). At Bollingen the 2-million-year-old man could emerge. He believed this "personality" stood outside time as we know it, and was eternal, existing in the collective unconscious. He had integrated Philemon so well that he seemed to have become him, the shamanistic, mediumistic, wise old man.

References

Bishop, Paul (1995) *The Dionysian Self: C. G. Jung's Reception of Friedrich Nietzsche*. Berlin: Walter de Gruyter.
Bishop, Paul (2014) *Carl Jung*. Critical Lives Series. London: Reaktion Books.
Campbell, Joseph (2002) *The Flight of the Wild Gander*. New York: New World Library.
Castillejo, Irene Claremont de (1973) *Knowing Woman: A Feminine Psychology*. Boston: Shambhala Publications.
Fortune, Dion (2003) *The Sea Priestess*. York Beach, Maine: Weiser Books.
Hannah, Barbara (1976) *Jung: His Life and Work*. New York: Putnam.
Henderson, Joseph (November 1977) Author's interview.
Jaffé, Aniela (1989) *From the Life and Work of C. G. Jung*. Eisdelen, Switzerland: Daimon Verlag.
Jung, C. G. (1965) *Memories, Dreams, Reflections*. New York: Vintage Paperbacks.
Jung, Emma (1985) *Anima and Animus: Two Papers*. Dallas, Texas: Spring Publications.
Osterman, Elizabeth (Fall 1977) Author's interview.
Ostrowski-Sachs, M. (1977) *Conversations with C. G. Jung*, trans. M. Marbury. Zurich: C. G. Jung Institute.
Samuels, A. (1986) *Jung and the Post-Jungians*. London: Routledge & Kegan Paul.

18
THE JUNGIAN WOMEN
An assessment

This work so far has dealt only with the first generation of Jungian women who knew Jung intimately and worked with him. They have now all passed on, most living to old age. I feel privileged that I was able to meet and to speak with so very many of them during my year at the C. G. Jung Institute in Zurich and on a subsequent trip there after I decided it was important to write their stories.

First, I must make the obvious point that all their work was done very specifically in the context of Jungian psychology in their written works. Most of them were analysts too and because of the privilege of privacy an assessment of their skill in that degree is impossible to gauge. So we have only their books and articles with which to assess them.

I will start with Emma Jung, the first "woman around Jung." It is unfortunate that her major work, born out of an interest in the Grail legends that was there even before she married Jung, is unavailable. Marie-Louis von Franz completed the work as *The Grail Legend*, supposedly at the deathbed request of Emma Jung. The only works of hers left are her two essays, published as *Anima and Animus*. Though her ideas on anima largely reflect Jung's own, she does introduce some of her own ideas as regards the archetype of the animus. According to Claire Douglas, "Emma Jung's more balanced perspective serves as counterpoint and corrective" (Douglas 2000, p. 152). Accordingly, "if woman does not meet adequately the demand for consciousness or intellectual activity, the animus becomes autonomous and negative" (Douglas 2000, p. 152). All of this is far from her famous husband's almost completely negative and fearful view of the animus. As far as the essay on the anima, she sticks closely to what Jung had formulated.

The case is much the same with Antonia (Toni) Wolff, Jung's guide through his own breakdown. Most of her work remained unpublished and available only through the libraries of the various C. G. Jung Institutes. Fortunately this has been remedied in the last couple of decades. The work we have is very much based on

Jung's own formulations, particularly his typology. Her feminine typology, which was structured on his *Psychological Types*, is very patriarchal, seeing women only in their relationship to men. However, it makes some very good observations about those types, particularly the Medial Woman. She was reputed to be an excellent poet, too, but none of her poems have survived.

As far as Linda Fierz-David is concerned, she used Jung's premises in one of her major works, *The Dream of Poliphilo*, but there are definite variations on his thought in her *Villa of Mysteries* that show more of her own thoughts and feelings about the feminine. Her view of the frescoes and their meaning as symbols of individuation is particularly feminine and deeply insightful as to woman's role in the world. I would thoroughly recommend it and Nor Hall's book on it for reading by all women, especially those involved in analysis.

In women such as Jolande Jacobi, Barbara Hannah, Esther Harding (with one major exception as we have seen, in her *Woman's Mysteries*), and Marie-Louise von Franz there is unquestioning use of Jungian concepts. Dr. Jacobi made Jung's psychology approachable by the general public, without his thanks, and we can be grateful to her for that. But in most of the women's work unquestioning acceptance becomes apparent, using fairy-tales, myths and even the Brontës, fitting them into sometimes rigid Jungian standard molds.

In the reading of many of these books by the Jungian women, one finds a rehash of old, tried, and not necessarily true Jungian constructs. The next generations of Jungian women appear to be breaking free of this. And I have a hunch that Jung himself would have become quickly bored with much of what had been written. Only a couple of the first-generation women had broken away even a bit from the animus idea, most notably author Irene Claremont de Castillejo, and his wife, Emma Jung.

In the past, feminist scholars were asking why no Jungian women and few Jungian men, with the exception of James Hillman, had questioned Jung's ideas. Naomi Goldenberg, who attended the Jung Institute in Zurich at the same time I did, wrote an excellent essay criticizing many cases where the very subjective selection of research material was used to "document preordained conclusions" (Goldenberg 1976).

One exception to this slavish following of Jung's ideas is *Woman's Mysteries* by M. Esther Harding, as already discussed. Her book is grounded in both history as well as psychology, and her research served as the basis for many of the books on the Goddess written in the 1960s, 1970s, and 1980s, and right up to the present.

The women around Jung were undoubtedly creative and intelligent, and, as noted, were themselves victims of the widespread prejudices about women that flourished strongly from the middle of the nineteenth century well into the twentieth and beyond to some extent. (It might be said, for the past 2,000 years.) None of them diverged very far from Jung's thought, nor deepened it noticeably. Not one of them ever saw fit to question any of his assertions about women and the archetype of the animus, nor added any conflicting research of her own, except Emma Jung and Castillejo. Certainly they would have been in a better position, if only because of their gender, to give empirical examples from their own psyches and those of their women patients. Throughout his writings, Jung himself makes several statements concerning the nebulousness of his basic material on the animus. For example: "Since the anima is an archetype that is found in men, it is reasonable to *suppose* [emphasis mine] that an equivalent archetype must be present in women" (Ostrowski-Sachs 1977). Reasonable to whom? Why not suppose that because man is born of Other (woman) that he must have reflection of her in his unconscious so as to help him subconsciously relate to the Other, while woman is born of Same (woman) and does not have this need in the same way? Goldenberg notes that Jung's followers "are prone to emphasize [the anima/animus model] to an even greater degree than Jung himself" (Goldenberg 1976). Of course, if I maintain too strongly that the concept of animus is erroneous, it is likely I'll be suspected of being animus-possessed!

In the final chapter we will see how succeeding generations of Jungian women and feminists have worked with this, while remaining Jungian.

The women around Jung and all serious people might listen to, and follow, the advice from Jung himself in the *Collected Works*:

> Therefore anyone who wants to know the human psyche ... would be better advised to ... bid farewell to his study, and wander with human heart through the world. There, in the horrors of prisons, lunatic asylums and hospitals, in drab suburban pubs, in brothels and gambling hells, in the salons of the elegant, the Stock Exchanges, Socialist meetings, churches, revivalist gatherings and ecstatic sects, through love and hate, through the experience of passion in every form in his own body, he would reap richer stores of knowledge than text-books a foot thick could give him, and he would know how to doctor the sick with real knowledge of the human soul.
>
> (Jung 1967, pp. 246–247)

References

Douglas, Claire (2000) *The Woman in the Mirror: Analytical Psychology and the Feminine*. Lincoln, Nebraska: iUniverse. First published Boston: Sigo Press, 1990.

Goldenberg, Naomi (1976) "A Feminist Critique of Jung." *Signs: The Journal of Women in Culture and Society* 2(2): 443–449.

Jung, C. G. (1967) *The Collected Works of C. G. Jung*, Bollingen Series 7: *Two Essays on Analytical Psychology*. Princeton, New Jersey: Princeton University Press.

Ostrowski-Sachs, M. (1977) *Conversations with C. G. Jung*, trans. M. Marbury. Zurich: C. G. Jung Institute.

19
SHE WHO REMEMBERS

Linda Fierz-David's marvelous book, *The Villa of Mysteries*, describes in detail the frescoes found in an ancient villa, now part of the UNESCO World Heritage Site at Pompeii. She outlines each fresco, depicting the stages of initiation of women in the ancient rites of Dionysus. As she describes the final one in the series – an older woman sitting on the throne of Mnemosyne, the Goddess of Memory – Fierz-David names her She Who Remembers. "She" is gazing out at the other frescoes of initiation, perhaps recalling her own. In my long, fifty-plus years of Jungian analysis and study, I seem to have arrived at that place myself, within the myth I am currently living. So it seems fitting somehow that this chapter, remembrances of my time at the Jung Institute in Zurich, should bear the name.

To a fervid Jungian student, the "mecca" of Jungian thought was the C. G. Jung Institute in Zurich, the original place where the Master himself had once taught, albeit with reluctance. Reluctance, as he felt going public with an institute was a tad too extraverted for an introvert such as himself and most of his followers. As I have written before, after dogged persistence one of Jung's few extraverted followers, Jolande Jacobi, talked him into letting the Institute come into being. Her argument had been that if Jung waited until he died, he would have no control. And so, soon after the Second World War, the C. G. Jung Institute for Analytical Psychology in Zurich, Switzerland, came into being. It was an imposing Victorian-era three-story building, covered in ivy. Its doors opened into a courtyard, not the street, which seemed to underline its very introverted beginnings.

In 1972, by the time I ventured from America to study as a young student in my thirties, the Institute was legendary. And most of the Jungian super-stars, including Marie-Louise von Franz, Barbara Hannah, Heinrich Fierz, and James Hillman, were alive and well and teaching, lecturing, and giving analytical hours. The halls, classrooms, and library of the Institute seemed to reverberate with the spirits of those who had gone before – students, teachers, and even Jung himself.

With trepidation and a feeling that an extraverted intuitive such as myself might be found unworthy and sent home to America, I arrived at the Institute at the beginning of the school year in October. How I came to get there at all is a journey in itself that began at the darkest of times for me personally – as all good, meaningful journeys seem to have to do.

Dr. Jung had already been gone for more than ten years. Yet, it was he who invited me to come.

In early 1971, I was diagnosed with cancer and told the treatment would have to be an intensive course of radiation. This was terrifying to me, the mother of two small children. I was so fearful I would not live to raise them and they were so terribly important to me. After six weeks of radiation treatment, three hospitalizations, and a marriage ready to come apart, I was left feeling depressed and hopeless.

To help raise my spirits, I enrolled in a class at the University of California, Berkeley, just a few blocks from home. They were offering "The Psychology of Jung," and though I had already had a five-year Jungian analysis I wanted to learn more of his intellectual system. At that time, Jung was still considered a bit of a renegade, and his work was not widely taught in mainstream universities in the United States. B. F. Skinner's behaviorism ruled the day and the colleges taught his psychology. But my Jungian analysis was proving to be very much the path I wanted to follow.

The course was taught by therapist Dr. Katherine Whiteside Taylor. She asked us to begin a journal during the course of the class, warning it would be turned in for her to read at some point during the class. I liked and trusted her so began to journal in earnest. It has since become a lifelong habit that I continue to find enriching. At the end of the semester she told us the University chose not to continue the next level of the class. I was crushed, but realized my living-room was large enough to accommodate a large class. I offered it to Dr. Taylor and the class so we could continue our studies with her, and all agreed it was a perfect solution.

One day, Dr. Taylor quoted something Dr. Jung had said, "You must go where the life is for you." Simple perhaps, but it struck me profoundly and I immediately withdrew from the proceedings to go over in my mind what had been interesting to me. Each thing failed to pierce my post-cancer depression until I came to "Europe." I felt a stirring in my solar plexus and a feeling of excitement I hadn't experienced in months. I shared my experience with Dr. Taylor. who looked at me with a wise smile: "My dear, if Europe, why not the Jung Institute in Zurich?" This took me completely by surprise. How could such a thing be possible? I had thought of going once the children were raised, if I lived that long. How could I possibly think of it now, just out of a major illness, two small children, separated from my husband, money tight? She somehow saw this all running through my thoughts, said she would write a letter of recommendation for me and she was sure my analyst, Dr. R. James Yandell, would too.

That night, I went over and over all the difficulties of such a trip, until finally I slept. I dreamed I was standing on a hillside overlooking a lake, which in the dream I thought was Lake Geneva. Dr. Jung stood next to me and said, "You must come to Switzerland, we have ancestors in common here." I awoke with a start. I had never had a dream of Jung before, and the dream was very real. I had not done any genealogy at that point and doubted I had any Swiss ancestors. (I have learned since that I do.)

I decided to throw the coins for the *I Ching*, for some unconscious confirmation. The hexagram came up whose first stanza states, "It furthers one to cross the water to see the Great Man." That did it. "Okay, okay. I'm going." I decided then and there to go, called the Institute in Zurich and got the English-speaking janitor in what was the middle of the night there. He advised me to call back later, when the staff was present.

I began selling my belongings and made reservations on the SS *France*, which was sailing for Europe at the end of September. I reserved tickets for my two children and me, and one for my mother to help care for the children during my studies. I was receiving child support and knew I could sublet my flat. This would be the extent of my funds in Zurich, a notoriously expensive city even then.

In September as our ship pulled out of the dock in New York, I was struck with anxiety and grave doubts about what I was doing. Then I remembered a line from a favorite writer, Lawrence Durrell, " every now and again one must put oneself in an extreme situation. You get a marvelous trampoline effect, saying to yourself, 'It's this or death!'"

Midway through the five-day journey I received a telegram from my brother telling me my beloved sister-in-law had died. In shock and anguish as we made our passage into the unknown, I realized my old life was truly ended and I was on my way to a new one.

The new life began with a bumpy lurch. After we'd left the ship, boarded a train for the last leg of our journey to Zurich, and were underway again, our train derailed. Thankfully no one was badly hurt. The children sustained scuffed but not badly damaged knees and a kind French doctor bandaged them, much to the children's delight.

We made it to Zurich by train in late afternoon, and as I stepped onto the platform I felt an enormous sense of homecoming, despite never having been there before. We took a taxi to our hotel in the old part of Zurich known as the Niederdorf, which has been there since the Middle Ages. The sense of homecoming was even stronger here. It was the district to which I would return again and again, finding solace and loving the ancient buildings and Grossmünster Cathedral within it.

First thing in the morning, I had to go to the Institute, to announce my arrival and register. I never did know her official title, but it was necessary for all new students at the Institute to meet with Frau Baumann as a prelude to becoming enrolled. (I later learned Jung's daughter was also a Frau Baumann at the Institute.) I entered her office with some trepidation and she began to question me rather mildly, asking what brought me there. When she found I had come to Zurich with my two small children and mother, she became instantly animated.

"What were you thinking? You don't have arrangements for living quarters? Do you know how expensive Zurich is?" With the barrage of questions and emotion hurled my way, I did something very uncharacteristic and burst into tears. All my defenses built up around the audacity of making such a journey in the face of my illness and treatment, separation from my husband, and the tragic death of my young sister-in-law, all came crumbling down.

Immediately, Frau Baumann began to spring into action. Before I left her office, she had inexpensive accommodations reserved for me and my family until the apartment she had already secured for us became available. She suggested a nearby French school for the children. I later learned that when Tibet fell to the Chinese, it was Frau Baumann who took charge of the Tibetan monks who had fled to Switzerland. So tending to the needs of an American and her family was a cinch for this woman of enormous energy and connections. I was and remain eternally grateful.

Once we were settled, I decided to sleep on the couch in the living-room and sublet the master bedroom to another student to help with our rent. I put up a notice at the Institute and one Stephen Martin applied. I liked him instantly. He reminded me of students in Berkeley with his wild hair and beard, and a gentle, thoughtful nature. He was an excellent artist and the youngest student at the Institute.

The folks at the Institute were confounded that so many young Americans were showing up there in the early 1970s. The revolutionary spirit of the 1960s had not shown itself in Zurich, and the Institute had been founded primarily with older adults in mind, people in mid-life or just beyond. Jung was a great proponent of the second stage of life being where one looked for answers to the big questions. It had not been the Institute's experience that young people could be or should be looking for such answers. However, we in America were just coming out of the counter-cultural age of the Flower Children, the Black Revolution, the Civil Rights Movement, the Women's Movement, and other cultural and political shifts of the late 1960s. It was the young who were asking the big questions in America and in the world in general. Stephen had been in college when he decided to come to Zurich. I was in my late thirties, still young by Jungian standards, and there were many others in their twenties who were there, and not all from America. The world was changing and we wanted to know our place in it. And of course, there were the very personal reasons of which most of us spoke only with our analysts.

One benefit of Stephen moving into the apartment was that he had an extraverted side, too. We began to accumulate a group of friends between us from throughout the world – Africa, America, Europe – mostly all in their twenties, who began to come to our apartment for dinner every evening. Each brought something to share for the meal. The talk was of the things we were learning at the Institute and our reading. It was all very stimulating and my children were indulged by all, too.

In order to attend classes at the Institute, it was highly recommended, even insisted upon, that one be in analysis. It was thought, rightly, that much of what was being studied would bring up issues that possibly were hitherto unknown to the individual. A class by Mary Briner on "Mothers and Daughters" brought up issues for all of us women as daughters and, for some, as mothers of daughters. One of the staff told me that the year before there had been a class called "Fathers and Sons," and frequently male students ran out and directly into the men's room, sometimes to lose whatever breakfast they had eaten. The courses at the Institute were psychologically based, of course, and some students who had started at the same time I did soon left the Institute. One had been a friend of mine in Berkeley, and he found the classes simply too hard on him, bringing up issues with which he did not want to deal. Another casualty was a Scandinavian friend who left without saying goodbye.

I had heard, before coming to Zurich, that Dr.med. Heinrich Fierz had made a study of tarot cards at Jung's suggestion, so I decided that, if possible, I would pursue analysis with him, as I had been studying the tarot and teaching its use for the past few years. I called and made an appointment. When I got there and was seated opposite him in what was actually a parlor in an apartment he used strictly for appointments, I told him of my interest in tarot. That I had been actually reading the cards professionally at a metaphysical center in San Francisco, and teaching classes in them. He pulled out a deck, asked me to shuffle them, then laid them out in a circle that represented the twelve houses of the zodiac. This done, he proceeded to give me a reading laying out all the complexes with which I had been struggling, card by card. I was amazed at his accuracy and suddenly felt like a rank amateur in the face of his knowledge and use of the cards. I decided on the spot I wanted to do my analysis with him. However, he said that he was completely booked with clients and it was not possible. He did have one appointment open the following week if I simply wanted to talk. I took it.

The following week, I showed up, we talked, and I once again said how much I really wanted to work with him. Again, he said it was impossible with his full schedule, but he had one appointment open the following week. I took it. When I showed up, we talked, and at the end I again said how much I'd like to work with him. He said fine, he had a permanent opening. I was in a daze when I left, then realized that as in many fairy-tales, I had asked the magical question three times and at last received the answer I wanted and needed. My analysis began. I was extremely fortunate being able to work with Dr. Fierz, and later, when I returned to Zurich to research material for my book on the women around Jung, he was most forthcoming about his late mother Linda Fierz-David and helpful about my desire to write about her.

Classes at the Institute were excellent and inspiring. What we soon learned was that there was a serious split at the core, with Marie-Louise von Franz, who had worked most closely with Jung in his later years, walking out and refusing to teach one year. Her bone of contention was that there was a course being offered on "Group Therapy," and von Franz categorically refused to allow such a thing at the Institute, saying Jung would not have countenanced it. Others in the Curatorium felt group therapy had merit and it was something in the air that should be recognized and looked into. So von Franz had swept out, and had taken some others, like Barbara Hannah, her housemate, with her. Some others of the first-generation Jungians had elected to stay, James Hillman among them. He was the youngest of that generation and taught a course that semester on "Animal Symbolism in Dreams." He was so popular and the class so large we had to hold it in another building entirely.

Dr. Hillman was a fine teacher, well informed and witty. Occasionally he could have a cold, biting temper and woe to the student who asked what Hillman felt was a stupid question. We were all intimidated by this and seldom asked anything but well-thought out enquiries. Even then he sometimes chose to use his cutting wit to answer, making us squirm in our seats, even if we were not the targets. In spite of knowing all this, one day at the main Institute, I was passing him on the stairs and happened to say, "I had an animal dream last night ... must be the class material." He cut me dead saying he didn't speak of class material out of class and brushed past with a sneer. I was very embarrassed as there were many others around.

Later that afternoon during my regular therapy session with Dr. Fierz, I told him of the encounter with Dr. Hillman and how humiliated I had felt. Now, I don't know what happened, as what is said in analysis is presumably confidential, but that evening, sometime after our communal dinner, there was a knock at my apartment door and when I opened it there was Dr. Hillman with his friend (and future wife), Patricia Berry, and a bottle of wine. "Mind if we join you?" he asked, smiling. I was so taken aback at him being there and being jovial and open that I can't remember what I said, but I did take them into the living-room, where many of the others had remained after dinner, and we talked and drank wine the rest of the evening.

The class he taught explored the meaning of the animals that appeared in our dreams and what they might have to say about us. He was very thorough and stimulating. One day he said that all of us had animal traits and that some of us might even resemble animals. "Even me. I'm sure that some of you can guess what animal I most resemble," he said. Immediately I saw his head and face replaced with that of a camel, but never dared to tell him, and he chose not to tell us.

Since von Franz had departed from the Institute, at least until some agreement could be reached, other professors and instructors were called upon to give classes. One was a Protestant minister from America who was to teach a class on Jung's typology, one of the mainstays of Jungian psychology. An entire book is devoted to the subject in Jung's *Collected Works* of course, and several of us were eager to sign up for the class. The first class was to be on extraversion. I looked forward to seeing just what traits I may be demonstrating as one who tested as an extravert, since I was in the minority in the Jungian world and indeed, it seemed, in Switzerland.

The professor began rather calmly, following Jung's text. Then he seemed to get worked up a bit and made the statement that extraverts were often alcoholic. I had not heard that said before, nor read it. Getting further worked up, he spoke of extraversion getting out of control, wildly, then made the astonishing statement, "And extraversion often leads to death!" This was said with great passion. There was a moment of silence, then we, the students, broke out in laughter, certain he had made the outrageous statement as a joke. It was not. None of us returned to the class again. I can only think the Institute had been rather desperate for teachers and had not evaluated this man very well.

Life in Zurich was one of discoveries. I loved the cold, crisp weather that set in shortly after we arrived in early October. The children, my mother, and I would walk the short distance from our apartment to the lake, where swans floated on the water. On foggy days, they would disappear for a moment, then appear some little distance away. Our apartment was very near the downtown area, as was the Institute, and the area was dominated by the Bahnhofstrasse, lined with luxury shops and one of our favorite stops, Sprüngli's café and bakery. We discovered that bakeries are very important in Zurich, and their displays announce which holiday is currently being celebrated or about to be celebrated. It was from the bakeries we learned that December 6 is as important as Christmas in Switzerland. This is the day when St. Nicholas, also known as Sinterklaas, visits and leaves candies and other sweet treats for good little boys and girls. For children who have been exceedingly naughty, he has a helper, Schwarzpeter, a chimney sweep dusted with soot who carries switches made of wood and a sack of coal. A very threatening figure, to be sure. In Austria, I've seen him depicted as a devil. One imagines that in Switzerland (where children are expected to remain quiet), it is those children who make noise all year who get the most attention from him via strikes with the switches and coal in their stockings.

In therapy, I mentioned this holiday to Dr. Fierz and he told me that as head of the Clinic and Research Center for Jungian Psychology, which incorporated the only Jungian mental hospital in the world, he would go into the woods a few days before the 6th and meditate, then transform into St. Nicholas. Fierz said he would meditate on what would be the best present for each of the patients in the hospital and also for staff. He invited my family and me to the annual party given at the Clinic.

So on that night, with two very excited children, my mother and I went to the Clinic, where a large room with plenty of chairs filled with patients and staff. Soon, there was a hush, and through a side door came St. Nicholas, accompanied by a rather benign looking Schwarzpeter. Dr. Fierz being tall and slender was perfect as the Germanic St. Nicholas in a long red coat with a hood edged in fur. My children were thrilled. One by one people were called to receive their gifts. For me, he had a woodburned brooch he said brought luck with money. He knew from what I had said in therapy that money was a constant issue. There was carol singing, and then it was time to go home. My children, Anna and Joshua, fell right into the custom and we have followed it ever since with the making of gingerbread and candies on December 6.

Magic, fairy-tales, myth. All are a part of the Jungian mythos and taken as seriously as everyday life, because Jung knew the power of myth had been forgotten for several hundred years in Western civilization. Myth was what really had caught me up in Jung's psychology, long before Joseph Campbell made his impression in his televised series about the power of myth in contemporary thought.

During my first appointment with my first Jungian analyst in Berkeley, Dr. John N. K. Langton, he asked, "Now tell me the story of your life." I was taken aback, being used to my earlier Freudian analyst, who would simply sit in silence until

I was so uncomfortable I would speak just to break it. So I began, aware of only fifty minutes to sum up the thirty years of my life up to that moment. When finished, I was further astounded when Dr. Langton got to his feet, walked to the window, then turned around and said "Why, you've been living the myth of Persephone!"

It is hard now to express the intensity of my feelings at that moment. It was as if a long tunnel had opened in the room, and I was one in a line of daughters, stretching back eons to ancient times. It took the burden of my psychological dependence on my mother, and put it in a perspective where I could stop blaming myself and feeling guilty. I knew the story of Persephone from my readings in Greek mythology, which had begun in childhood. The daughter of Demeter, the Earth Goddess, she was out picking flowers with friends one day when the ground opened up and Hades, the Lord of the Underworld, came up from the deep and kidnapped her, taking her to his Kingdom of the Dead beneath the earth. Demeter knows only that her daughter is lost and she cannot find her. In her sorrow, she lays the earth waste. Finally all life is threatened to the point where Zeus, Father of the Gods, tells his brother Hades he must return Persephone to her mother. Crafty Hades feeds her some seeds of the pomegranate. Exactly three seeds, which means she must spend three months of the year with him and the rest of the year return to her mother. And that is why we have the three months of winter. Later, in my feminist studies, I was to discover an even earlier version of the myth, where Persephone learns of the terrible loneliness of the dead and voluntarily spends part of the year with them in the Underworld with the disapproval of her mother.

Discovering my personal myth and knowing it to be psychologically true helped me begin the long journey to discovery of self. In Zurich, working with Dr. Fierz, I could feel a new myth was emerging and it was incumbent on me to discover just what it was.

Very often, when I would begin to speak, Dr. Fierz would say, "I don't feel like doing analysis today. Let me tell you a story about Dr. Jung." At first this was disconcerting, as I usually came with an agenda which I wished address and receive feedback on. Gradually though, I learned that when he did this, at the end of his story I would find it spoke to the very issues with which I was concerned.

Once when I came for my hour, I told him I was feeling so terribly burdened with responsibilities for keeping a roof over our heads, for my children and their well-being, for my mother, for my studies. Dr. Fierz looked at me and said, "Why, that means you must go out and be a gypsy for a few days and not handle anything." I jumped a bit in my chair and told him I just saw an image in my mind of someone handing me a pot of hot soup, and me refusing to take it. The pot shattered on the floor and all the soup spilled all over. "Oh, there will be accidents," he smiled benignly. After the session, I remembered that as a child, I had always, on Halloween, chosen to wear the costume of a gypsy. I wondered if that had been an unconscious choice to relieve me of the burden of my symbiotic relationship with my mother, which threatened so often to smother me?

One of the classes that turned out to be a favorite of mine was Sandplay, the therapy devised by Frau Dora Kalff, which took place at her house a short distance from Zurich, in Zollikon. The house was very old. At first glance I thought the number over the door, 1485, was her address. But no. It was the date of the first construction of the house, during an era when more than fifty Gothic churches were built in the parishes around Zurich and secular buildings included less ornate but still notable influences of the grand Gothic style. As Frau Kalff wrote in her book *Sandplay*, "My house was constructed hundreds of years ago on rock; its rooms were not built and shaped by yardstick and compass, but grew according to natural laws" (Kalff 1980). It had been completely redecorated on the inside, filled with thangkas and other Tibetan pieces, surrounded by modern, simple furniture. I later learned that she, too, had made friends with the Tibetan monks who had fled when the Chinese invaded their homeland, and occasionally met with the Dalai Lama.

Frau Kalff herself had gone to Jung years before at the suggestion of his daughter, to share her thoughts concerning art therapy, including the concept of Sandplay. The basic idea is that the therapist provides a choice of two sandboxes of specific dimensions, "man-size," as Frau Kalff said, standing on supports. One of the sandboxes is filled with damp sand that can be molded, and the other with dry sand. Along the walls of the consulting room are several shelves that hold a variety of miniatures. These are anything from small houses, castles, shops, people in a variety of guises from everyday occupations such as policemen, firemen, housewives, and so forth, to more exotic folk like elves, princesses, knights in armor. There is always a large selection of animals, too, from wild to domestic. Her workroom, which was situated in the basement of her house, had several hundred such figures.

When Frau Kalff began her practice, it was only with children. However, it was not long before she began to see that in terms of Jung's ideas on the process of individuation, this therapy could be of help at any age. For adults, it gave them a safe and protected space in which to play, in addition to its healing powers. In therapy, the client was asked to choose one of the sandboxes in which to work, and to set up a scene within it. Once it was completed, the therapist asked the client to speak about it in any way they wish. For our first class, she showed a film featuring a variety of scenes that had been set up by former, unidentified clients. As I watched, I saw immediately that the scenes foretold what the therapy was to deal with, and what was going on psychologically with the client. I was very impressed with the process and with the diminutive, self-taught woman who had discovered and invented the process.

Jung had been very encouraging and impressed with her work, and many Jungian analysts use the process as an adjunct to their own practice. I looked forward each time to her sessions and a few years later took more classes with her at the University of California, Santa Cruz, in a long seminar. Later, I had a small Sandplay practice of my own in Northern Nevada.

Another course with implications for my future was a seminar on creative writing, given by a newcomer to the Institute, Dr. Sam Eisenstein, who was a university professor from southern California. He had decided he wanted to become an analyst and had come to Zurich with his wife, Betty, a photographer who had interviewed and documented various dance groups in India. We became friends and I registered for the course, which was being offered in the attic of the building in which the Institute's *Spring Quarterly* was put together. At the time, it was occupied by Dr. Hillman.

Sam and Betty and I became good friends, and Sam began to have the dream of producing the first literary journal ever at the Institute. He worked hard on it, and many of us contributed stories for the first edition. It debuted as *Garuda: A Journal of the C. G. Jung Students' Association, Zurich*. The editors were Sam, his wife Betty, and Roger Woolger. In the Editor's Note, it is explained that Garuda is both a spiritual and chthonic god, who unites heaven and earth as King of the Birds, but holds a snake in his mouth. Stephen Martin did a lovely, whimsical drawing for the opening pages. Many future Jungian analysts contributed stories and poems. In addition to a short story and a book review, my contribution was to arrange the first student dance ever at the Institute, where we would hold an auction to pay for the printing of the journal. The auction offerings included analytical hours with some willing analysts at the Institute. I approached Dr. Hillman, Dr. Fierz, Dr. Luigi Zoya, and Professor Dr. P. Rupp and all agreed to donate their hours. In addition, Dr. Fierz's wife contributed an hour-long geomancy reading.

The dance itself was interesting in many ways, not least because there had never been such an event at the Institute before (or maybe since). The night of the dance and auction, Marie-Louis von Franz came, along with Barbara Hannah and a few of the women of the Jungian old guard. They sat like chaperones on the sidelines. After the auction, the rest of us danced. One friend, who was a lovely, youngish woman from Cuba married to the racy British spy novelist Adam Diment, was also a great dancer. She was also exotic-looking and a very sexy lady. As she danced wildly to the rock music, her peasant blouse slipped off her shoulders. I went up to her at one point to warn that Dr. von Franz was looking askance at her, at which my friend threw back her head, shook her assets, continued dancing, and announced loudly, "I don't geeve a fock!"

All in all, a very successful event, yet I don't believe there was ever another dance after I left, perhaps due to a paucity of extraverted Americans.

After the dance and auction, life continued much as before at the Institute, as we went into the spring semester. There were rumors that Marie-Louise von Franz, or "Ma-Lou" as she was known, might soon be back to teach, as the Institute had caved on the question of group therapy. For myself, I believed Jung had been such a progressive thinker that he might have accepted group therapy, but with his own spin on it.

Meanwhile, in the midst of all the intellectual work at the Institute, the children, my mother, and I continued our exploration of Zurich. The children always begged to be taken to Grossmünster Cathedral and down into the crypt to see the centuries-old statue of Charlemagne there, which looked a little terrifying. They were thrilled with it, finding it quite "spooky." I would tell them the history of the place, perhaps a legend. Charlemagne was out hunting with his dogs and at the top of the hill, the dogs began pawing at the ground, digging away, when they uncovered the bones of three Christian martyrs. On the spot, Charlemagne decided to build the cathedral there to honor them. It was begun in the eighth century and there it still stands. Many years later, researching genealogy from my mother's side, I learned that along with a few million other living human beings, we are direct descendants of Charlemagne, who is my thirty-ninth great-grandfather. I wish I had known at the time to tell the children. Years later the cathedral became the key setting in one of my novels, *Dark Ritual*.

In analysis with Dr. Fierz, I discovered my new myth was that of survivor. Unfortunately we could find no myth containing a woman as central character. Only the story of Odysseus, his survival of the Trojan War, and his subsequent wanderings and adventures on his way home seemed to provide a back story to what I was experiencing after cancer surgery/treatment, loss of my sister-in-law, and move to Zurich. This myth was to continue for several years as I struggled to make a life for myself as a single woman with children.

One day in a therapy session, Dr. Fierz made a surprising offer to me. He proposed that he and I together teach a class at the Institute in the coming summer session on the mythology behind the tarot. To say I was surprised and pleased would be an understatement. Such an offer was beyond my wildest dreams. But alas, it was a short-lived dream as, soon after, von Franz decided to return to teach in the summer, which left no room in the schedule for our course, and that was that.

It was only a month or so later that another surprise came; this one darker. I received a letter from my soon-to-be-ex-husband that he could not continue to afford two households and he was coming to take the children and me back home to Berkeley, where we would somehow have to put our marriage back together. The letter was followed rapidly by his arrival in Zurich. I was anguished. I went to Dr. Fierz to ask his advice. Maybe I *should* go back into my marriage, and try again to make it work, for the sake of the children? Dr. Fierz nodded sagely and said, "Yes, you could do that. But you must realize he will never, ever change." (At the time it seemed a harsh judgment, but as it turned out later, Dr. Fierz was right and we eventually divorced.) As I would not be able to continue my studies in Zurich, Dr. Fierz had waiting for me, when I returned the next day for a final session, a certificate he had made and signed on the stationery of the Clinic and Research Center for Jungian Psychology. It states, among other things, that Maggy Anthony has

> continued training with us as a psychological social worker. She has an excellent attitude in meeting and helping people, she has a good knowledge of Analytical Psychology, and in discussing psychological problems she can also handle groups. We think that for an analyst, she can be a helpful collaborator, and that she is also able to work independently.

He signed it as Director of the Clinic. I was very, very touched and honored he would do such a thing so personally. I thanked him profusely and asked how I should continue my studies in America. He stunned me by saying he thought I shouldn't go back to school, but instead be the guru he felt I was! Having to leave Zurich, I felt I had failed in some way. The thought of him saying he believed I was a guru was stunning indeed. I left with a teary goodbye.

It was so very hard, saying goodbye to a life I had come to love. It was the only time in my life I had experienced a real sense of community and the ideas shared by that community. And the sense of freedom I had achieved there was also hard to leave.

On departure, a friend had given me a book by Dr. C. A. Meier, one of my professors at the Institute, *Healing Dream and Ritual*. It was of great interest to me as it told of the ancient healing temples of Asclepius, the Greek God of Healing, where people would come to be cured of various illnesses. Sufferers would be put in incubation, or a sleeping mode, to await a dream that would foretell a cure. The dreams would be interpreted by temple priests and when a healing dream took place, the patient was free to go home. That this mode of treatment was successful is proved by the hundreds, perhaps thousands of stone tablets found near the sleeping temples (*asclepeions*), carved with thanks to the gods of the temple for the cure of their various complaints. This was what I was reading on the voyage home.

It interested me greatly. And it was to provide one of the strangest demonstrations of synchronicity I have ever experienced.

After we boarded the ship in Genoa, instead of heading for the US the ship pulled into Naples, where the crew decided on a one-day strike. All passengers had to disembark for the day. Since we were so close to Pompeii, we decided to take the children there for the day. It was off-season, so we had the site practically to ourselves.

As we strolled down one of the ancient streets, a guard appeared and made a beckoning gesture at us to follow, but it became obvious it was at me he was pointing. Hesitantly I followed, and he led me to a low, locked gate leading to a group of roofless buildings and then to a building with only three walls standing. On the inside of each wall were ancient frescoes. Each showed a person reclining as if sleeping, while another figure stood by. The guard looked at me and said in Italian, "Sonno, sonno." And made the gesture of sleeping, with closed hands, his head leaning against them and his eyes shut. I got it: This was one of the Greco-Roman healing temples and a place of incubation. I was astonished. I had left the *Healing Dream and Ritual* book on the ship. How could this man, this guard at Pompeii, know this was of particular interest to me? Bewildered, I looked around at all the frescoes, and indeed, this place was a sleeping temple. Finally, the guard looked at his watch and made the gesture of eating … it was his lunch hour. I went back to my waiting family and wondered at the marvelous synchronicity of this kind guard somehow knowing this one thing in Pompeii was what I needed to see.

This reassured me completely: Though my time in Zurich was over, another personal journey of discovery was about to begin.

Reference

Kalff, Dora M. (1980) *Sandplay: A Psychotherapeutic Approach to the Psyche*. Boston: Sigo Press.

20
INTO THE FUTURE

The battle of the animus

> The animus remains sacrosanct; tended like a folk icon from medieval times, kept polished and in good repair even by heretics who doubt its validity and plot secretly, like mad Reformers, to replace it with another.
>
> *(Cowan 2013)*

These words, written first in the 1990s and not published until 2013, are by a present-day woman Jungian analyst. I think we are now seeing attempts to change and materialize in the work of modern Jungian women analysts in this century some concepts that no longer fit. And fortunately, the baby is not being thrown out with the bathwater ... by that I mean these women still identify as Jungians, but have the courage and intelligence to recognize that Jung was a man of his times and of his own personal psychology, and because of that his psychology will have theories and ideas that no longer play out in modern times, especially as regards the animus.

Throughout the preceding pages, in the lives of the first generation of women around Jung, we have seen where the definition of animus did not serve them well. And it was, perhaps, their own birth within the Victorian era that kept them from contradicting, or even enlarging upon, the sexist concept of the animus. Of course, their attachment and projections upon Jung also played a role. "[T]he powerful aura surrounding Jung scarcely allowed anyone to dream of criticizing him or taking him down from his pedestal" (Fuller 2017, p. 67).

Though there have been many prominent Jungian women analysts in the twentieth century following Jung and the first generation of Jungian women, very few of them have taken his concept of the animus to task for the way in which it limits women, including themselves. As has been noted by a recent feminist/Jungian analyst, "Building on the foundation provided by Emma Jung and Toni Wolff, their lives and their devotion to Carl Jung become, consciously or not, the model for how to be a woman and a Jungian" (Fuller 2017, p. 67).

Beginning in the 1980s the voices speaking out against the concept of anima/animus became louder. In an article/review by Claire Douglas, she makes a good point about the general thrust of the three books reviewed.

> I agree with the authors when they wish to do away with the animus insofar as it is used as a put-down and to blame women.... The concept is valuable when ... the animus is used descriptively as if to say "Here look at this, look at the way the patriarchy has been internalized within you."
>
> *(Douglas 1986, p. 12)*

The books which she was reviewing were *For Women Growing Older: The Animus*, by Jane Wheelwright; *Change of Life* by Ann Mankowitz; and *Feminist Archetypal Theory: Interdisciplinary Re-visions of Jungian Thought* by Estelle Lauter and Carol Rupprecht. These were just the tip of the iceberg of books and articles coming out in the 1980s concerning Jung's concept of the animus and the feminine and how it no longer seemed to serve women. Other women writing on similar themes at the time were Nora Moore, M. A. Matoon, Barbara Greenfield, Kay Bradway, and Polly Young-Eisendrath.

More recently, another Jungian woman analyst has put it succinctly, addressing directly the needs and values of this new century. "Abandoning the notions of anima/animus does not mean that the basic tension between these two poles cease to exist, but rather that de-genderizing, an intellectual project of our time, demands we renew the metaphors behind the notions" (Paris 2017, pp. 132–133).

So we look to works coming out in the twenty-first century for even more clarifying of concepts that don't serve us as women. Such authors as Susan Rowland, Leslie Gardner, Lyn Cowan, Cheryl L. Fuller, Coline Covington, and others are continuing this process and many of them are Jungian women analysts of the new generation.

And so we go into the future, reworking some concepts to bring them up to date and possibly disposing of others which no longer serve us or have meaning in our lives. We leave it to these Jungian feminist analysts and writers to do this with us.

Jungian women of the twenty-first century

In early 2017, my friend John Roth attended a three-day seminar at the Pacifica Graduate Institute in Santa Barbara, California. What most impressed him was a lecture by Dr. Patricia Arah Ann Taylor. He learned she was a member of a group of women calling themselves the Black Divas of Depth Psychology, and further, that they had all contributed essays to a book, *Seeing in the Dark: Wisdom Work by Black Women in Depth Psychology*. He immediately phoned me knowing of my interest in finding the new generation of Jungian women leaders and innovators. He was able to provide her email address and I contacted her, followed by a telephone interview in February 2017.

The first question I asked Dr. Taylor was, "What drew you to Jung's work?" She replied she had been studying psychology, mostly behavioral, and did very well in it but felt the need for something more.

> At Pacifica, I saw that depth psychology connected us all as one unit: mankind. In dreams, symbols, and metaphors, it all came together for me. From my work in depth psychology, I feel unstoppable. I have a connection that is powerful – rooted in all life: rocks, trees, earth, minerals, all of it. I think I may have had that from birth but the study of depth psychology brought it all forward again.
>
> All this I use in my work, teaching teachers who teach children who have been marginalized, called, in general, Special Education. I teach them to see how their students are rooted, not to see them as broken, or as circus acts, etc. To look at them from a psychologically rooted place themselves. Who are *you*, speaking to students? How can you help them recognize their gifts?
>
> *(Taylor 2017a)*

Dr. Taylor comes from a long line of educators, from a great-grandmother who lived for 105 years and was a member of the North Carolina Bird Clan Cherokees, who married an emancipated slave and moved to Oklahoma. They had to take on the education of their eleven children themselves as, though black children were allowed to attend school, Indian children were not.

She also speaks proudly of her grandmother, who wrote, but never thought of publishing. Then a local newspaper had a writing competition on the theme, "What Does it Mean to be a Grandmother?" She wrote a paper, sent it in, and won first prize.

Dr. Taylor knows the value of words and tells her students to study words and the meaning of words and their origins, to see new stories in them. She is married to Michael Meade, the mythologist and storyteller, "who knows the value of words," she said.

In the book *Seeing in the Dark*, she contributes an essay, "My Legacy and the Legacy of Enough in the Workplace: Moments of Clarity from a Crone of Color." And a poem, "A Candle for My Father," which is a devastating one prefaced with a biographical introduction which could be universal, containing the sentence, "I light a candle to all the horrible fathers, the violent ones, the abusive ones, the abandoners, the weak, the selfish ones, the ignorant ones" (Taylor 2017b, p. 53). Dr. Taylor is Chair of the Special Education Program at the University of Laverne.

Another of the Jungian Divas, Kimberly L. Howell, MBA, Ph.D., came to Jung's psychology in another way. She spoke of a recurring dream in which she was underwater, and under the rubbish in that water. She would awaken, choking. After reading Jung's work on synchronicity, Dr. Howell had the dream again, only this time in her dream she relaxed her body and bobbed to the surface where she saw Monarch butterflies, trees, and an ocean. "The place I saw was Pacifica and so I went there and worked toward my Ph.D." (Howell 2017a). She had experienced body dysphoria, being diagnosed in her early twenties. She writes of this in her essay, "Re-Visioning Hollywood's Gods: The Pantheon of Celebrity."

> The language of the psyche is deeply steeped in image, particularly fantasy images tethered to the messages in celebrity magazines and culture, and they send a soul eroding signal that the skin in which we were born, and the accompanying changes of aging, deem women invisible or unworthy in many regards.
>
> *(Howell 2017b, p. 61)*

Dr. Howell's essay speaks to our obsession with celebrity and the images that we take on in this. She uses Marilyn Monroe in this chapter and her status as a Hollywood Goddess and writes of "The Unwitting Greek Tragedy of Marilyn Monroe" (p. 63). Dr. Howell's career has taken her to Silicon Valley, where she works as a corporate trainer. She said she incorporates Jungian concepts in this work but tempers the terms, translating them into corporate language. She also teaches privately, conducting body image workshops.

Dr. Sharon Johnson, who is the editor of *Seeing in the Dark*, and lecturer in the Department of Africana Studies at California State University, Northridge, wrote in her response to my queries that she was drawn to the psychology of Jung when she read a book by John Sanford, *The Kingdom Within: The Inner Meaning of Jesus' Sayings*, which is a depth psychology interpretation of biblical scripture. After that she began to read more Jungians and Jung's own writings.

When asked if she sees her Jungian work having an impact on the future of psychology, she wrote:

> I hope so, particularly among African-Americans. My work always includes reclamation. For well-documented reasons about how African-Americans have been treated historically by white practitioners in the medical and mental health fields, we generally have a distrust of being probed physically and psychologically. Add to that the fact that followers of Jung (and Freud, for that matter) have failed to emphasize that Jung (and Freud) gleaned much of his psychological insight from ancient African practices, particularly Ancient Egypt. We perhaps are more aware that Europe monopolized the formation of these practices into a formal discipline: "Psychology," but many African-Americans don't realize the genesis of these practices or the work of African-American practitioners such as Dr. Edward Bruce Bynum, who substantiates that the Unconscious is African. Through teaching the practices, such as dream work and active imagination, to African-American audiences, I aim to reclaim it by putting us back in touch with our own psycho-spiritual genealogy and heritage.

Dr. Johnson went on to write:

> I am finding that the lens of depth psychology is my preferred approach to all of my work: creative, spiritual, educational. There is no personal or professional work that can't benefit from depth psychology examination. It expands, deepens, and reveals wherever it is applied.
>
> *(Johnson 2017a)*

Additional colleagues and authors among the Black Divas of Depth Psychology include Dr. Marcella "Marcy" De Veaux, a depth psychologist and associate professor in the Department of Journalism at California State University, Northridge; Alisa Orduña, community development practitioner and doctoral candidate at Pacifica Graduate Institute; and Dr. Sherrie Sims Allen, a depth psychologist, author, and life coach.

Their entire book, *Seeing in the Dark*, is a strong new contribution to the literature of depth psychology. Johnson writes in her Introduction, "Carl Jung – identified as one of the fathers of modern Depth Psychology – emphasized to his mentor and colleague, Sigmund Freud, that analytical psychology must not be a solely Eurocentric discipline" (Johnson 2017b, p. xv). And this important book and its contributors look to remedy that trend, only recently acknowledged by the International Association for Analytical Psychology, which issued a formal "acknowledgement and apology concerning Jung's attitudes and writings on persons of African heritage," on May 9, 2016, on which Dr. Johnson also comments in her Introduction.

All this put me in mind of Jung's trip to East Africa in 1925, which has been widely cited by Jungian writers and by Jung himself, particularly in his *Memories, Dreams, Reflections*. One insight in particular struck me. "I could not guess what string within myself was plucked at the sight of that solitary black hunter. I knew only that his world had been mine for countless millennia" (Jung 1961, p. 255).

Throughout Jung's account of his five-month trip he stresses the familiarity to him of certain events and places. All this, sixty-two years *before* we were presented with DNA evidence that we all come from the first Mother, the African Eve of East Africa. "We now know we are all Africans. Jung instinctively understood that he had arrived at his ancestral home … he was stating what is now (but not in 1925) an established fact of paleontology: *Homo Sapiens* originated in East Africa" (Burleson 2005, p. 62). Yes, Jung also brought with him many of the common mistakes and arrogances of thinking of his contemporary European society, but also opened himself to the inner truths of his African discoveries. "For Jung, 'primitive' referred to an undifferentiated layer of the human (and animal) psyche which had evolved out of the ubiquitous unconscious" (Burleson 2005, p. 16).

Reading this I thought of Dr. Taylor's teaching of the study of words and their origins. Actually the word "primitive," which has come to have such negative connotations, originally referred to original or primal cause, and, before 1400, the original ancestor. All this according to *Chamber's Etymological Dictionary*. It did not become a term of derogation until Victorian times, when it was used as an excuse for colonization and slavery. "It is not an overstatement, as Togovnick suggested, that this experience set 'the future course of Jung's career, contra Freud'." And, "It was here, on the Athi Plains, Jung found his *raison d'être*, his 'myth'" (Burleson 2005, p. 16). All this had begun for Jung in the same year he made his trip to New Mexico and spoke with the Hopi elder, Mountain Lake, becoming aware of the poverty within the spiritual life of Western culture. Jung saw that the need and attendant morning ritual of the Hopis to get up and help the rising sun ascend was so essential to their well-being; and then in Africa, he witnessed similar rituals and spiritual thinking. "Jung was the first to formulate the problem of modern man as mythlessness" (Edinger 1984, p. 13).

Seeing in the Dark and other important contemporary works continue to address and remedy this.

Jungian women in the first half of life

Seattle therapist Satya Doyle Byock, MA, LPC, is one of the first women depth psychologists to specialize in analysis in the first half of life. A good part of this must be attributed to her own struggles as a young woman. As she told me in conversation, "I was restless all my life. My parents were supportive, so when I was in college and existentially dissatisfied, I took a year leave. I went to Sri Lanka for a time, then returned." Still restless, Doyle Byock went to Bogotá and worked with prisoners there. Once again she returned home and then saw that a major tsunami had struck, so she went back to Sri Lanka to assist. Back home again, her mother gave her a copy of Thomas Moore's *The Care of the Soul*, which interested her. However, it was the gift of *Memories, Dreams, Reflections* that hit the mark. She felt, as so many of us did when reading it, that all she had been interested in and feeling was expressed in that book. So after obtaining her bachelor's degree, she went to Pacifica School of Graduate Studies and completed her master's in analytical psychology. She then began to research Jungian views on the first half of life and found there was very little available. Mostly early adulthood was regarded and written about as a time to concentrate on careers and family.

As Doyle Byock states in her article in *Psychological Perspectives*, within Jungian psychology, "Like the forgotten middle child, the first half of life is mentioned in passing for the sake of comparison to the other stages, rarely identified with its own characteristics or praised for its unique value" (Byock 2015).

She attributes this partially to analytical psychology being developed in the first half of the twentieth century, when life was very different from what it has become in the past seventy-five years. "For a generation raised on a heavy diet of apocalyptic news worldwide … the call to return to the unconscious beckons earlier than in the past" (Byock 2015).

And so, Doyle Byock's practice is focused on those in their twenties and thirties. She concludes by writing that "a psychology oriented toward the soul can help young adults learn that their symptoms are natural responses to an unbalanced education and a world in chaos" (Byock 2015).

Her activism has not stopped there. She has recently founded the Salome Institute of Jungian Studies in Portland, Oregon, stating that the Institute is for the study of classical Jungian psychology and its modern application. At present the Institute's offerings include lectures and classes on a variety of topics: the *I Ching*, astrology, symbols, racial understanding, gender equality, and a host of others. She states, "I see the Institute as in the Fourth Wave of feminism."

References

Burleson, Blake (2005) *Jung in Africa*. New York: Continuum Press.
Byock, Satya Doyle (2015) "The Inner World of the First Half of Life: Analytical Psychology's Forgotten Developmental Stage." *Psychological Perspectives: A Quarterly Journal of Jungian Thought* 58(4): 399–415.
Cowan, Lyn (2013) "Dismantling the Animus." *The Jung Page: Reflections on Psychology, Culture and Life*, October 27, www.cgjungpage.org/learn/articles/analytical-psychology/105-dismantling-the-animus.
Douglas, Claire (1986) "The Animus: Old Women, Menopause and Feminist Theory." *San Francisco Jung Institute Library Journal* 6(3): 1–20.
Edinger, Edward (1984) *The Creation of Consciousness*. Toronto: Inner City Books.
Fuller, Cheryl L. (2017) "Emma Jung's Pen: Jung, Feminism and the Body." In *Feminist Views from Somewhere: Post-Jungian Themes in Feminist Theory*, Leslie Gardner and Francis Gray, eds. Abingdon: Routledge, pp. 56–70.
Howell, Kimberley L. (February 2017a) Author's interview.
Howell, Kimberley L. (2017b) "Re-Visioning Hollywood's Gods: The Pantheon of Celebrity." In *Seeing in the Dark: Wisdom Works by Black Women in Depth Psychology*, Sharon Johnson, ed. New York and Malibu: Malibu Press, pp. 59–78.
Johnson, Sharon (March 2017a) Personal communication.
Johnson, Sharon (2017b) "Introduction." In *Seeing in the Dark: Wisdom Works by Black Women in Depth Psychology*, Sharon Johnson, ed. New York and Malibu: Malibu Press, pp. xii–xxx.
Jung, C. G. (1961) *Memories, Dreams, Reflections*. New York: Vintage Paperbacks.
Paris, Ginette (2017) "Ideas a Feminist Should Leave Behind." In *Feminist Views from Somewhere: Post Jungian Themes in Feminist Theory*, Leslie Gardner and Francis Gray, eds. Abingdon: Routledge, pp. 132–133.
Taylor, Patricia (February 2017a) Author's interview.
Taylor, Patricia (2017b) "A Candle for My Father." In *Seeing in the Dark: Wisdom Works by Black Women in Depth Psychology*, Sharon Johnson, ed. New York and Malibu: Malibu Press, p. 53.

21

THE *HIEROS GAMOS*

The old alchemist stands amid the tables covered with bubbling retorts and bottles of mysteriously colored liquids. At his side, working beside him each step of the way, is a woman who goes about her work, occasionally checking with the old sage. In the air there is a sense of tension, and a feeling that many unseen beings are present in the ancient laboratory … ancestors, archetypal forces.

The alchemist has been working a lifetime at this process, trying first one set of ingredients, then another, conferring with his colleague. Finally it is ready. And the carefully chosen components have gone into the athanor, made for the working of the *magnum opus*. Essences of many plants, flowers, herbs, minerals included. Today they put in the extract of sunlight, tonight, this moment, it will be the full moon's silvery rays.

The hands of the woman tremble as she parts the curtains. It is the only sign that she may be nervous. A full moon is temporarily hiding behind a wisp of blue-grey cloud. Then slowly its silver beams of muted light shine into the room and deep into the open door of the athanor which the old man has placed to receive the moon essence. He now adds a drop of some other substance his *soror mystica*, the sister of his soul, has handed him.

The athanor glows and turns red. Inside, the process has begun and there is no stopping it now save at the loss of everything. All night the process continues, and it is only by the softened noises within the tightly shut furnace, and the heat emanating from it, that one knows something is happening. There is no one in the room to witness it. Both the old alchemist and his female partner have vanished.

Finally there is a change in the athanor. It ceases to glow or make any sound. From out of the shadows, comes a solitary figure: a tall, slender person who goes with youthful vigor straight to the small oven and without hesitation, opens the door. Strong smooth hands reach inside to draw out something, and as they do so, a sinuous jeweled snake coils around one wrist until its head meets its tail, which it then puts in its mouth and seems to doze off. The hands withdraw the Work … the Work that would pass unnoticed by most … a large, smooth stone. Just a stone, but bearing within it the opposites contained in eternal balance, rotating to the celestial rhythm so precisely tuned that to the untrained eye the effect is one of stasis.

The figure with its bracelet of jeweled serpent holds the stone aloft with reverence, and in the light of it we see the figure is neither that of the old alchemist nor of his *soror mystica*, but a being, complete in itself, containing both. The *magnum opus* has taken place. The androgynous being has completed the *hieros gamos*.

The ultimate goal in Jungian analysis, or the process of individuation which it aims to facilitate, is the *hieros gamos* or Divine Marriage. Jung borrowed the term from medieval alchemy, and his last great work, *The Mysterium Coniunctionis*, was devoted to its study and psychological interpretation. To put this complex operation into the simplest terms possible, the *hieros gamos* is the process by which one's opposites are brought together to form a single androgynous being psychologically.

This takes place within an individual's psyche when the opposites are integrated. It is the marriage of the conscious and the unconscious and the resulting totality brings about a "new" person: a psychic rebirth of sorts. Of course, it is the ideal, a life-enhancing vision of the possibilities of psychic union.

Claire Douglas has pointed that, "It is of relevance to Jung's theory of the feminine that Jung largely excludes the female half of the alchemical pair, and denies the relevance of alchemy to feminine experience" (Douglas 2000, p. 99). She goes on to quote Jung, "The alchemical texts were written exclusively by men and their statements are therefore the product of masculine psychology" (Douglas 2000, p. 99) But she argues against this that "in the eleventh edition of the Encyclopedia Britannica (1910–11), an edition of Jung's era, the source of alchemy is given as originally an area of women's knowledge, of matriarchal possession" (Douglas 2000, p. 99). Once again, the ignoring of the female contribution.

I believe that the early women around Jung used their relationship with him as a sort of acting out of the *hieros gamos*. They felt a "marriage" to him at a very deep level and perhaps that is the reason most of them remained unmarried. It would be difficult for a mere man to compete with such a figure, who reached these women psychically in such a meaningful way. The theme shows up frequently: in Hilde Kirsch's dream and Jung's interpretation of it; in the dream of Jolande Jacobi; and even in the facetious nickname of another of the Jungian women who was referred to as the "bride of Christ."

To extend this further, we might say that the body of work that came from these women is the child or product of this union, which is perhaps why it takes so much from Jung and does not achieve any significant expansion of his thoughts, particularly on the feminine.

Whatever the reason, the life-sustaining nature of the deep connection is seen in the long, productive lives of these women. In each case, their relationship with Jung seems to have enabled them to live their lives at a very deep level, and their dreams and visions sustained them after the death of the man who they felt had taken them seriously for the first time.

Reference

Douglas, Claire (2000) *The Woman in the Mirror: Analytical Psychology and the Feminine*. Lincoln, Nebraska: iUniverse. First published Boston: Sigo Press, 1990.

APPENDIX 1

Jung's birth chart by Philip Culjak[1]

> There are many analogies which can be made between the horoscope and the character disposition. There is even the possibility of certain predictive powers.... The horoscope seems to correspond to psychic archetypes.
>
> *(Brau 1977)*

> We are born at a given moment, in a given place, and we have, like the best wines, the quality of the year and the season which witness our birth. Astrology claims no more than this.
>
> *(Brau 1977)*

Carl Gustav Jung was born at the time when the Sun was in the sign of Leo and the Saturn-ruled sign of Capricorn was rising at the eastern horizon of his birthplace, Kesswil, Switzerland.

Astrologically, the rising sign indicates how the world sees and views the individual, as well as the way in which the individual tends to see, view, and interact with his or her environment. The Sun indicates the ego and the potential within the individual to continue to be and to become whatever it is the essence of that individual to be and become.

The Saturn-ruled sign of Capricorn portends early limitations, real or imagined, felt by the person with such a sign as Capricorn rising. With this, there is a sense of inadequacy which tends with age, experience, and introspection to dissipate.

The ruling planet of Jung's rising sign is in the sign of Aquarius, in the 1st House of his natal chart. This position further reinforces his feelings of limitations and inadequacy, and suggests that his father, represented by his Saturn, in the unique sign of Aquarius, would be a major influence in Jung's view of the world.

The Sun, in the sign of Leo, placed in the 7th House, denotes tremendous potential for self-fulfillment and individuation. The creative potential is tremendous, but it requires cooperation and partnership (7th House symbolic meaning).

"Long live the king." The energy is dynamic, solar. In honor of the ruler Sun, the energy instinctively desires public acclaim and approval. As a fixed sign, Leo stands high on a pedestal and surveys the surrounding fields. Magnanimity, warm-hearted generosity are given to the people, as long as the pedestal is high and dominance assured. Yet assumption of a lofty position can lead to the downfall of any shining leader unless he produces what he promises.

> The energy distribution can manifest as an inspiring leader or a show-off. The range is as great as the energy potentials are vast. The self-reflection can be so true and vivid that arguments, suggestion, and ramifications never see light. In Leo, the dimensions of theatricality are very strong. Applause is the way to a Leo heart. The square similarity with Taurus (two fixed signs) would clash: the energies have different natures but similar modes of expression. Maybe "likes" do repel as in a magnet! Overwork and overachievement are difficulties for the Leo, depending on the need shown in the rest of the horoscope. The heart and spine are parts of the body ruled by the Sun in Leo.
>
> (Tyl 1973)

Jung's personality is seen through the Moon in the sign of Taurus, which is placed in his 3rd House. The Moon symbolizes, in its most basic sense, self-preservation. It represents the emotional nature of the individual, and chart analysis stands for the instincts, the unconscious, the mother, and women in general. It is indicative of the anima and is associated with memories, dreams, and imagination.

The Moon in the sign of Taurus is exalted and increases the individual's capacity to nurture not only the Self, but others as well.

We have, within the Ascendant, the Sun and the Moon, the basic ingredients of the potential for Carl Gustav Jung. A Leo Sun, energetic, creative, and proud. A Taurus Moon, with his self-preservation tied to a practical, earthy, and stubborn emotional nature. Finally his view of his world seen through his Capricorn Ascendant – reflecting limitations felt, ambition, desire for success, and recognition through achievement.

For those ingredients to mature, we must look to the aspects formed by the planets to those very important indicators – Ascendant, Sun, and Moon. It is within the aspect formations, house placements, and signs that the dynamic tension needed for the potential of the individual to be realized and fulfilled are to be found.

Looking at Jung's natal chart as a whole, it becomes clear that there are two groupings of planets, a 1st House Saturn in Aquarius trine a 9th House Jupiter in Libra, with a Mars in Sagittarius in his 11th House, forming a sextile to both Saturn and Jupiter is the first group.

The second group consists of a 3rd House placement of Neptune in Taurus forming a square aspect with the 7th House Leo Sun, a Moon–Pluto conjunction from the 1st to the 3rd House with the Moon in square aspect to Uranus in the 7th House in the sign of its detriment, Leo.

What enables the energies to flow and fulfill themselves is Saturn square the Moon–Pluto conjunction from the 1st to the 3rd House and Jupiter square both Sun in Leo (7th House) and Venus in Cancer in the 6th House.

The essence of the Self requires nourishment to flourish. The early years of an individual are symbolized by the Moon as Mother and by Saturn as father. Jung's Saturn Moon square indicates stresses felt through the parental interaction with himself and between themselves. The needs of the child are felt as not being met by either parent. Saturn (father) in the sign of Aquarius suggests a unique or bizarre interaction, and the nurturing Taurus Moon (the mother) suggests a potential for smothering, with the possibility of creating a greater alienation between father and son.

In time, the Moon enables Jung to nourish himself and aids his understanding of his mother and of women in general. It is the feminine in himself (the anima) with which he is in touch. However, Saturn, symbolically the father and Shadow, remains to haunt him.

> The Shadow is symbolized by Saturn, the dark angel or Satan, and here we see that which we fear and that which we repress with the greatest emotional intensity, that is those things which we project and dislike most in others because we cannot bear to accept them as parts of our own nature.
> ...
> As the child needs to be accepted by his parents, those parts of the Self which do not meet acceptance, or which the child believes will not be accepted by his parents, become repressed. This dark, unacceptable side is the Shadow.
>
> *(Szanto and Acker 1987)*

The impetus to fulfill the ambition of Saturn and gain the acceptance Jung needed is aided by the conjunction of Pluto–Moon in the sign of Taurus in the 3rd House of his natal chart. It is the self-nourishing emotional nature combined with the willpower of Pluto creating the push to succeed. (Moon–Pluto conjunction square Saturn.)

The planet Pluto symbolizes the mysteries of life – sex, birth, and death. It is the potential to regenerate and transform that which is no longer useful in the individual's life. Pluto also symbolizes will, and placed in the sign of Taurus:

> Pluto ... revolutionizes the Communication System in general and mental attitude undergo drastic changes. ... The intellect (lower mind) and perceptions are forced into deeper channels of thought and feelings and made to backtrack until the proper vehicle of transition becomes clear.... The need

to cry out – by speaking, writing (or ranting) – becomes overpowering and with Pluto in the 3rd House one appears to be fated to stand alone.... Sense impressions are sensitized: memory patterns reach deep into the subconscious vortex and sense of conscious evolution motivates the behaviour.
(Lowell 1973)

Moon conjunct Pluto:

> Natives with this conjunction have intense feelings and are strong willed.... They may display psychic and occult tendencies and a leaning toward a subtle emotional domination of the surroundings. They can have a compelling influence over other people. They are open to superphysical realms of manifestation.... Their interest in spiritualism or matters pertaining to life after death can make them aware of those who are disincarnate. There is also a tendency to let the past die and to create entirely new bases for emotional experience. Natives are fearless and willing to take risks, and Pluto, ruling the principle of elimination, death, and rebirth, causes them to seek extreme and drastic changes in their lives. They may deal drastically with their families, bringing about sudden changes in the domestic sphere. Sometimes they alienate women by their brusqueness and tendency to be overbearing. Whether this conjunction is expressed in creative genius or in destructive emotionality will depend on the aspects made to it and the horoscope as a whole.
> *(Sakoian and Acker 1973, pp. 287–288)*

In order to understand the importance of Jung's Moon in Taurus, and to gain further insight into his personality we look to the Moon–Uranus square from the 3rd and 7th Houses. Uranus symbolizes the potential of the individual to utilize freedom. Moreover, the energy of this planet indicates sudden and unexpected events; it refers to friendships, hopes, and humanity.

> Uranus in the sign of Leo indicates a generation of people who seek freedom in love and romance. Their ideas about courtship and sex may depart from traditional moral standards and they are likely to believe in free love. Uranus in Leo can give strong willpower and creativity in the arts and sciences as well as potential for original kinds of leadership. People with this position seek to create a unique type of expression in order to be outstanding in their endeavors. They can develop new concepts in art, music and the theater. Rather than conform to the standards of the society they live in, they prefer their own standards. However, there is a danger of egotism in this position... Hence they should get involved in matters of social or universal – rather than personal – concern. These people can be stubborn, and they have difficulty compromising or cooperating with others. If Uranus is afflicted in this sign, they will insist on having their own way to the extent that they will completely refuse to cooperate.
> *(Sakoian and Acker 1973, p. 202)*

Uranus in the 7th House brings the symbolic meanings of that house, such as marriage, partnerships, close personal friendships, contacts with the public, and legal contracts into the area of one's life experiences. Unexpected and sudden changes are certain to occur as the tendency for freedom within these restraints is strong.

To see how the essence of Self (Leo Sun) is tested, we look to the developmental tension of Sun–Neptune square. In the sign of Taurus, Neptune as the ruler of Pisces, a water sign, loses its receptive qualities to earthy practicalities, and indicates the potential for inspired thought utilized in nurturing. Neptune as the ruling planet of the natural 12th House symbolizes the ideal of compassion toward all living things without reward. Neptune in the house of the rational mind (3rd House) presents the potential for delusion or inspiration. The self-deception possibility would be very great without the strong Saturn, which Jung has. And it is the combination of practical, self-nurturing will with inspired thought processes which drives the ambition (Saturn) and gives, through Saturn, the fixity of purpose to transform himself.

Another aspect of tension is Jupiter in Libra in the 8th House in an "out of sign" square to the 7th House Leo Sun. The 8th House is the natural house of the sign Scorpio, ruled by the natural ruler of Scorpio, Pluto. Jupiter symbolizes the potential of the individual to attain wisdom, through travel, education, and experience. Jupiter in Libra indicates the areas of experience involved in the tension of the aspect. It is basically partnerships, cooperation given and received. As Leo Sun (king) is given cooperation and, in the face of refusal, his emotional powerhouse explodes (Moon conjunct Pluto and Moon square Uranus). The lesson to be learned is both one of giving cooperation and curtailing the false pride a Leo Sun has a tendency to express. The self-discipline of Saturn must be brought to bear if the ego is to be fulfilled in its quest for evolutionary enfoldment.

The 6th House placement of Venus in the sign of Cancer is also a source of dynamic tension through its square aspect to Jupiter in the 8th House in Libra. There is much feeling and sensitivity with Venus in the sign of Cancer. The natural ruler of Cancer is the Moon and Venus is the ruling planet of Taurus. Astrologically, these planets are potentially in mutual reception, allowing their energies to manifest more positively.

Venus through its natural rulership of Taurus, the ruler of the natural 2nd House, is associated with the following areas of experience: the individual's sense of values, the ability to accumulate wealth, attraction to and by others, the aesthetic sensibilities, and personal comfort.

The 6th House symbolizes service to others, personal health, and employment. The sign governing the natural 6th House is Virgo (ruled by the planet Mercury), which is positioned in the 6th House in the sign of Cancer and thereby dignified.

Within the square aspect of Jupiter and Venus, the tension that develops is that personal expansion (Jupiter) suffers when the lack of cooperation given is perceived, thereby resulting in personal discomfort (Venus). The natal chart potential is for this aspect to utilize the discipline of Saturn and the judiciousness of Jupiter to transcend the negative results.

Mercury conjunct Venus indicates the potential for Mercury's thought processes (accidently dignified in the 6th House) to be expressed with great understanding and sensitivity in regard to service to others and through his profession. It is Jung's emotional giving that draws women to him; giving, perhaps, that which he felt he wished to receive.

> Your gentle and easy-going personality is an asset in most professions, but you might find it difficult to cope with the abrasive elements of close and direct competition. This possibility should be taken into consideration when choosing a profession. It is better to work alone or with a small group of people so you won't have to worry about troublesome competition.
> (Pelletier 1974, p. 77)

The Leo Sun sextile the Taurus Pluto

> shows that you are fully aware of the intensity of your will. Deep within, you understand that you can accomplish almost anything you want without too much resistance from others. You realize that without knowledge, however, you can't fulfill your destiny.... Your ability to communicate your thoughts is so great that others are mesmerized by your words. This ease of communication is your greatest asset. You also have a flair for handling other people's resources, and you easily inspire their confidence in your abilities. Because your talents are so precious, you owe it to the world, as well as to yourself, to make them available to everyone.
> (Pelletier 1974, p. 77)

The energies of Pluto in the sign of Taurus in the 3rd House flow positively and boost the ego in service to others.

The sextile of the Taurus Moon and Mercury–Venus in Cancer symbolizes the potential for sensitive and nurturing communication within service to others, which facilitates regeneration and transformation of thought processes and perceptions of others.

How individuals strive to become empowered and fulfill their potential requires energy as symbolized by the planet Mars.

Jung's Mars is positioned in the 11th House of his natal chart, placed in the Jupiter-ruled sign of Sagittarius. (Sagittarius is the natural ruler of the 9th House with the planet Jupiter as its ruler.) Mars represents the manner in which a person asserts himself; it is applied energy relating to all forms of activity, whether it be in competition, work, or sex. The energy of Mars tends to express itself as an all-out effort when placed in the 11th House, especially in regard to the 11th House areas of hopes, wishes, recognition, and humanitarian concerns. In the sign of Sagittarius, the fire of the energy does not burn with the impulsiveness of Aries, nor with the brightness of Leo, but has a fervor of its own.

The sextile between Saturn and Mars symbolically gives the individual the mental stamina to lay the foundations and prepare for success. The Jupiter–Mars sextile symbolizes the potential for the mental aspirations through higher education, travel, and philosophy. Each of these sextile aspects reinforces the trine aspect between Saturn and Jupiter.

The Saturn–Jupiter trine symbolizes the easy flow of energies between Jupiter (8th House home of the mysteries of life and other people's resources; the natural house of Scorpio, ruled by Pluto) in Libra, the sign of partnerships and cooperation given and received, and Saturn in the 1st House, representing the self as opposed to others.

Within the trine, there is ambition (Saturn) furthered by expansion through the use of other people's resources (Jupiter in the 8th).

Carl Jung has eight planets in the northern hemisphere of his natal chart, one, Saturn, is in an air sign; three, Neptune, Moon, and Pluto, in earth signs; two, Mercury and Venus, in water signs. These placements indicate, especially with Capricorn as a rising sign with Saturn in his 1st House, that he is considered to be an introvert with an emphasis on intuition and feeling.

Venus, ruled by the Moon (natural ruler of the 4th House of early beginnings), is in a trine aspect to the rising sign and indicates a loving, perhaps doting mother and is in a square aspect with Saturn and indicates a tension within the father–son relationship. This is most probably due to the tension Jung feels through his square of Saturn–Moon, indicating tensions between his mother and father.

Jung's perception of his world finds its core in these tensions. He is able to see the duplicity and contradictions inherent in human beings, and he turns within himself to resolve those tensions.

The strength of his essence, with his Sun in Leo, shows that his high level of creativity will take place through the tensions of early life, which stimulate his introspection and give impetus to his naturally ambitious nature. He "will," with the Moon–Pluto conjunction, make sense of his life through a high degree of intuition afforded him (Neptune–Moon–Pluto) in the 3rd House of rational thought, combined with his solar creativity so pronounced in the sign of Leo.

The intellectual energy needed for Jung's evolutionary progress is given to him through his Mars in the sign of Sagittarius, the higher mind of thought, education, and travel. This planet in sextile aspect to both Saturn and Jupiter helps Saturn's ambition through the easy flow of energies between persistent and unique Saturn in Aquarius and Mars' intellectual energy. Mars, in turn, aids Jung's personal expansion, with the sextile aspect to Jupiter. The trine aspect between Saturn and Jupiter encloses the sextile, creating a dynamic potential for successful striving.

For the release of energies, we have, on the one hand, the necessary developmental tensions brought about by the Moon and Saturn "pushing the buttons" of Jung's ambition, which stimulate both the Saturn–Jupiter trine and Mars sextile Saturn and Jupiter. On the other hand, we have Jupiter square the Leo Sun. The need for recognition and approval is found through determined and creative intellectual accomplishment.

Jung worked his way through the above complexities, starting with the desire to understand himself and then others, and ultimately came to understand himself.

Note

1 Carl Gustav Jung's birth information was obtained from Brau (1977), who gives a birth time different from Marc Edmond Jones, who gives it as 7.20 p.m., in his *Guide to Horoscope Interpretation*. The author wishes to thank the late astrologer and dear friend Philip Culjak for his generous work, comments, and interpretations of Jung's chart.

References

Brau, J. L. (1977) *Larousse Encyclopedia of Astrology*, trans. Helen Weaver and Allan Edmands. New York: McGraw-Hill.

Lowell, Laurel (1973) *Pluto*. St. Paul, Minnesota: Llewellyn Publications.

Pelletier, R. (1974) *Planets in Aspect: Understanding Your Inner Dynamics*. New York: Schiffer Publishing.

Sakoian, F. and Acker, L. S. (1973) *The Astrologer's Handbook*. New York: Harper Row.

Szanto, G. and Acker, L. S. (1987) *Astrotherapy: Astrology and the Realization of the Self*. London: Arkana/Routledge & Kegan Paul.

Tyl, Noel (1973) *The Principles and Practice of Astrology*, vol. 1. St. Paul, Minnesota: Llewellyn Publications.

APPENDIX 2

Timeline: C. G. Jung and the Jungian women

1875	Birth of C. G. Jung (1875–1961), July 26, in Kesswil, Switzerland.
1887–1899	Gymnasium years.
1900	Begins work at Burgholzli Clinic.
1903	Marries Emma (1882–1955).
1904	Couple moves into Burgholzli.
	Sabina Spielrein (1885–1942) arrives as inpatient in Burgholzli.
	Jung initiates professional correspondence with Sigmund Freud.
1906	Personal relationship with Freud begins.
1909	Spielrein causes scandal claiming she and Jung are lovers.
1910	Toni Wolff (1888–1953) begins analysis with Jung. Tension begins between Jung and Freud.
1911	Weimar Congress begins. Jung and Emma act as chaperones for Toni Wolff at Toni's mother's request. Spielrein does not attend; sends excuse.
1912	Final break with Freud.
1913	Edith Rockefeller McCormick (1872–1932) arrives in Zurich, escorted from America by Jung.
	Beginning of Jung's confrontation with the unconscious. Visions begin. Relationship with Toni intensifies.
1914	Writings in Black Books begin.
1915	Red Book begins.
1916	Psychological Club founded.
	Interaction with Dadaists in Zurich begins.
1920	Sennen Cove, Cornwall, lectures. Meets Dr. Eleanor Bertine (1887–1968).
1922	Dr. M. Esther Harding (1888–1971) founds London Psychological Club.

1923 Talks at Polzeath, Cornwall. Meets Dr. Kristine Mann (1873–1945).
1924 Jung in Taos, New Mexico. Meeting with Hopi elder, Ochiway Biano.
1925 Travels to Africa.
1927 Mary Foote (1871–1968) arrives in Zurich.
1928 Barbara Hannah (1891–1986) arrives in Zurich.
1930 Wolfgang Pauli (1900–1958) appears in Jung's life.
Meets Olga Fröbe-Kapteyn (1881–1962).
1933 Jung travels to Palestine and Egypt with Hans Fierz-David. Attends first Eranos conference.
Marie-Louise von Franz (1915–1999) begins working closely with Jung on alchemy.
1937 Jung and Fowler McCormick travel to India.
1939 Jolande Jacobi (1890–1973) escapes Nazi-occupied Vienna, arrives in Zurich.
1942 Mary Mellon establishes the Bollingen Foundation with Yale University to publish Jung's *Collected Works*.
Sabina Spielrein dies.
1948 C. G. Jung Institute founded in Zurich.
1952 Toni Wolff dies.
1955 Emma Jung dies.
1961 C. G. Jung dies.

AUTHOR BIOGRAPHY

Maggy Anthony studied at the C. G. Jung Institute in Zurich, Switzerland and the Zurich Clinic and Research Center for Jungian Psychology. She has lectured widely in New York and throughout the western United States on Jungian psychology, dreams, mythology, women's spirituality, and journaling. In addition to previous editions of the present volume, she is the author of several works of fiction, including two mystery series, and a play about the life and death of Marilyn Monroe. Raised in San Francisco, Anthony has also lived in Rio de Janeiro, Zurich, Paris, the Cotswolds in England, Berkeley, Eugene, and New York. She currently resides in northern Nevada, where she was a family therapist at St. Mary's Medical Center/Maclean Center for Addictions and Behavioral Health for more than fifteen years before retiring to travel and write. She may be reached at grammadragon@gmail.com.

INDEX

active imagination 43, 61–2, 77
alchemy 33, 34, 44, 64, 120–2
Amman, Fraulein 5–6
analytical psychology 1, 38, 42–3, 81, 85–6, 93, 118
Analytical Psychology Club, New York 52, 58
Analytical Psychology Institute, New York 55, 119
anima 1, 3, 13, 25, 26, 28, 45, 92, 98, 100, 114
animus 19, 25, 81, 93–4, 98, 100, 113–14
Anthony, Maggy 101–4, 105–6, 107–8, 109–12, 115
archetypes 11, 25, 61, 94, 98, 99–100
Arp, Jean 40, 41, 42
Arp, Sophie *see* Taeuber, Sophie
art 42, 44, 45, 62
astrological charts 26–7, 123–30
"A Study in the Process of Individuation" (Jung, 1934) 57

Bailey, Ruth 19, 82
Bancroft, Mary 34, 80, 85, 86–7
Baumann, Frau 103–4
Bertine, Eleanor 52, 54, 56–7, 58, 93
Binswanger, L. 7
Bishop, Paul 92, 94
Black Books (Jung, n.d.) 14, 42
Black Divas of Depth Psychology 114–17
Brazil, ceremony in 53–4
Briner, Mary 86, 105

Burgholzli Clinic, Zurich 9, 15, 22
Byock, Satya Doyle 118–19

Campbell, Joseph 79, 95, 107
Castillejo, Irene Claremont de 94, 99
celebrity 116
C. G. Jung Institute for Analytical Psychology, Zurich 6–7, 37, 64, 71, 101–2, 103–7, 110
Clinic and Research Center for Jungian Psychology, Zurich 107

Dada 40, 41, 44
Dadaists 40–1, 42, 43, 44
depth psychology 115, 116, 117
Dionysus 7–8, 9, 48, 61, 94, 95
Douglas, Claire 35, 54, 77, 78, 81, 98, 114, 121
Dream of Poliphilo, The (Fierz-David, 1987) 47–8, 99
dreams 32, 49, 52–3, 93, 106, 122; Anthony 102–3; Elliott 89; Fortune 74; Howell 115–16; Jacobi 69, 121; Jung 13, 18, 19, 24, 31, 35–6; Kirsch 88, 121; Osterman 82–3; Spielrein 23; von Franz 64, 66
Dulles, Allen 86, 87

Eisenstein, Sam 109–10
Elijah 2, 3, 31, 97
Elliott, Lucile 88–9
Eranos 59, 60, 61, 62, 71
Ernst, Max 44

fairy-tales 64, 65, 99
fantasies 23, 24, 31, 32
feminine 1, 13, 48, 49, 91, 99, 114, 121
Fierz-David, Hans 47
Fierz-David, Linda 6, 33, 34, 46, 47–8, 49, 95, 99, 101
Fierz, Heinrich 96, 101, 105, 106, 107, 108, 111
Firth, Violet *see* Fortune, Dion
Foote, Mary 84–6
Fortune, Dion 61, 73–4, 75–6, 94
Freud, Sigmund 8, 14, 16, 21, 22, 25, 26, 91, 8, 17, 19, 22, 25, 30, 31, 38, 41, 42, 14, 15, 16, 17, 30; *see also* Jung Carl Gustav; *see also* Jung Emma
Frey-Rohn, Liliane 7, 71
Fröbe-Kapteyn, Olga 59–61, 62, 71, 73

Gnosticism 43
Goldenberg, Natalie 99, 100
Grail legend 17–18
Grail Legend, The (Jung and von Franz, 1980) 64–5, 98
Great Mother 11, 13, 61
group therapy 64, 105–6, 110

Hall, Nor 48–9, 99
Hannah, Barbara 49, 66, 80–1, 89, 91, 96, 99, 101; active imagination 43; group therapy 64, 105–6
Harding, M. Esther 48, 51, 52, 54–5, 57, 58, 93, 99
healing temples 112
Henderson, Joseph 34, 53, 62, 95; about Harding 52; about Jacobi 7, 70
Hermetic Order of the Golden Dawn 43
Hesse, Hermann 43–4
hieros gamos 121
Hillman, James 99, 101, 106
Hinkle, Beatrice 57, 58
Hitler, Adolf 59, 87, 88
Hopi Indian people 41, 118
Howell, Kimberly L. 115–16

I Ching 69, 87–8, 103, 119
individuation 39, 49, 57, 60, 99, 109, 121

Jacobi, Jolande 6, 7, 32, 68–72, 99, 101, 121
Jaffé, Aniela 6, 31
Johnson, Sharon 116–17
Joyce, James 38
Jung, Carl Gustav 6–7, 22, 26, 30–1, 91; astrological chart 27, 123–30; dreams 13, 18, 19, 24, 31, 35–6; Emma 14, 15, 16, 17, 19; Eranos 60, 61; Freud 8, 17, 19, 22, 25, 30, 31, 38, 41, 42; Grail legends 18; mother 3, 11, 12–13, 92; patients 8, 9, 15, 17, 22, 68, 95, 96; Salome 3, 92; tuberculosis 46–7; views on women 1, 3, 7, 8–9, 91, 92; visions 31, 42–3, 66, 92, 97
Jung, Emilie Preiswerk (mother) 3, 9, 11, 12–13, 92
Jung, Emma (wife) 14–15, 16–18, 19, 25, 31, 34, 64–5, 92, 94, 98, 14, 15, 16, 17, 30; *see also* Freud Sigmund; Wolff, Toni (Antonia) 15, 16, 26, 30, 31, 35
Jungfrauen 1, 6, 61
Jungian psychology 2, 8, 9, 11, 12, 31, 38, 45, 70, 74
Jungian women 1, 3, 6, 34, 91–4, 95, 98–100, 113–15, 121–2

Kalff, Dora 83–4, 108–9
King Stag (play, Gozzi, 1762) 41
Kirsch, Hilde 87–8, 96, 121

Langton, John N. K. 108
Long, Constance 52, 57, 58
Lowenfeld, Margaret 83
Luhan, Mabel Dodge 84, 85

McCormick, Edith Rockefeller 37, 38
mandalas 42
Mann, Kristine 37, 52, 54, 56, 57, 58, 93
Martin, Stephen 104, 110
Masks of the Soul (Jacobi, 1976) 71
Meier, C. A. 7, 16, 35, 71, 112
Memories, Dreams, Reflections (Jung, 1965) 3, 11, 15, 26, 31, 41, 117
Morgan, Christiana 77–8
Murray, Harry 77–8
myths 17–18, 99, 107–8, 111

Nazis 69, 86, 87, 88
Neumann, Erich 60, 71

Oppenheim, Meret 44
Osterman, Elizabeth 81–3, 97
Otto, Rudolf 60

patients 15, 17, 26–7, 38, 68, 95, 96
Pauli, Wolfgang 65–6
Persephone 108
Philemon 3, 35, 97
Preiswerk, Samuel 12
primitive 42, 117–18
psyche 9, 12, 93, 117, 121

psychoanalysis 22, 25, 91
Psychological Club, Zurich 5–6, 33–4, 37–9, 40–1
Pueblo Indian people 41

Rauschenbach, Emma *see* Jung, Emma
Ravenna mosaics 33
Red Book, The (Jung, 2009) 1, 2, 3, 14, 15, 18, 24, 34, 42, 45, 92, 97

Salome 2, 3, 31, 92, 97
Salome Institute of Jungian Studies, Portland 119
Salome (play, Wilde, 1894) 2
Sandplay Therapy 83, 84, 108–9
schizophrenia 29, 32
Schlegel, Erika 33–4, 40, 41
second personality 11, 12, 96
Seeing in the Dark: Wisdom Works by Black Women in Depth Psychology (Johnson, ed., 2017) 114, 115, 116, 117, 118
Sennen Cove seminar (1920) 51–2, 57
shaman 45, 93, 95
Siegfried 23, 24
Society of Jungian Analysts, San Francisco 89
Society of the Inner Light 73, 76
Spielrein, Sabina 3, 9, 15, 21–4, 25–6, 27–8
Surrealism 44

Taeuber, Sophie 40, 41–2
tarot cards 105
Taylor, Katherine Whiteside 102
Taylor, Patricia Arah Ann 115, 117

Theosophy 59
transference 9, 17, 22, 34
tuberculosis 46–7

Valkyries 1
Villa of Mysteries, Pompeii 48
visions 32, 77, 78, 122; Jung 31, 42–3, 66, 92, 97
Visions Seminars, The (Jung, 1997) 77, 78
von Franz, Marie-Louise 18, 49, 63–7, 94, 98, 99, 101, 110, 111; active imagination 43; alchemy 33, 34; group therapy 64, 105–6

Weimar Congress (1911) 15, 25, 30
Wheelwright, Jane 9, 34, 89
Wheelwright, Joseph 8, 34, 68, 89
Whitney, Elizabeth 89
Wolff, Toni (Antonia) 3, 6, 16, 19, 25–6, 29–31, 32–6, 71, 92, 98–9, 15, 16, 26, 30, 31, 35; *see also* Jung Emma; patients 17, 34–5, 86
"Woman in Europe" (Jung, 1927) 7, 58, 80, 91–2
Woman's Mysteries (Harding) 52, 53, 54, 99
women 1, 7, 17, 52, 65, 79, 81, 91–3, 100; animus 93–4; Jung views on 1, 3, 7, 8–9, 91, 92
women patients 8, 9, 13, 15, 17, 22, 68, 100
Women's Dionysian Initiation: The Villa of Mysteries in Pompeii (Fierz-David, 1988) 48, 99, 101
word association 22
World Technique 83